Marlborough
on the Menu

Copyright © 2008 recipes & food text Jan Bilton
Copyright © 2008 food photography Jan Bilton
Copyright © 2008 wine matches and wine text Belinda Jackson
Copyright © 2008 Introduction and additional text Michael G. Ryan
Copyright © 2008 Irvine Holt Enterprises Ltd

Design: Debbie Morgan, Art Tank Ltd,
22 Kowhai Drive, Te Kouma, Coromandel

First published in 2008 by Irvine Holt Enterprises Ltd,
PO Box 5183, Springlands, Blenheim 7241,
Marlborough, New Zealand

ISBN 978-0-9597594-5-7

Many thanks to:
The Restaurant Association of New Zealand – photographs pages 17, 25, 79, 123
Destination Marlborough – scenic photographs
Jill Van Angeren – saffron flower photograph
Wine Marlborough – wine trail map
Trudy Frew – kitchen assistance

Printed in China through Bookbuilders

Marlborough
on the Menu

Jan Bilton
Food

Belinda Jackson
Wine

Michael G. Ryan, Editor

Irvine Holt

4

CONTENTS

Exotic saffron

Whether you've got an appetite for fine food and fine wines, eco-adventures or just kicking back and relaxing in spectacular surroundings – or all three – you'll find something to suit your taste on Marlborough's menu of attractions.

New Zealand's sunniest region is also the country's premier wine producer and the irresistible temptations of world-class Sauvignon Blanc, award-winning Chardonnay, Pinot Gris, Riesling, Gerwurztraminer and Pinot Noir partnered with gourmet food can easily lead to a life of guilt-free self-indulgence as many Marlburians will happily confirm.

Of course, if the sybaritic lifestyle starts to wear you down you can take a break. Experience the bewitching world of the Marlborough Sounds – cruising, kayaking, diving, fishing or swimming with dolphins, the choice is yours. Tramp the magnificent Queen Charlotte Track; go mountain biking on spectacular trails; or treat yourself to the thrills of whale watching off the Kaikoura coast.

Captain James Cook was the first wine lover to visit Marlborough when in 1770 he claimed the South Island for King George 111, named Queen Charlotte Sound, and toasted Her Majesty's health with an entire bottle of wine. (Perhaps he thought he was quaffing a Marlborough Sauvignon Blanc.) Cook also released pigs and his legacy lives on – wild pork matched with Pinot Noir is a local favourite.

As all wine lovers and foodies know there is more to Marlborough than just tasting the terroir – superb though it is. The region is also a culinary paradise. As several leading winemakers point out in the following pages, there is no more pleasurable experience than savouring fresh local gourmet foods – Pacific King salmon, green-lipped mussels, oysters, scallops, crayfish, farmed venison, wild game, specialty cheeses, stone fruit and berries to name just a few of the delights – matched with palate-pleasing wines.

And for those who want to sample the freshest of the fresh here are some choices – buy fish still tasting of the sea on Picton's wharf; pick your own strawberries on the outskirts of Blenheim; and check out Blenheim's Farmers' Market (October to April) for organic treats. The philosophy driving New Zealand's second oldest market is simple, 'Fresh, quality, local products – direct from the farm gate to your dinner plate.'

Marlborough hosts a number of events to celebrate its finest wines and cuisine including the Wine Marlborough Festival (February), the Havelock Mussel Festival (March) and the Kaikoura Seafest in October.

Marlborough on the Menu is your invitation from chef and food writer Jan Bilton and wine expert Belinda Jackson to treat yourself to the best the 'top of the south' has to offer.

FRESH SALMON

Marlborough Sounds salmon begin life in the perfect environment – hatched in clear South Island mountain streams before being transferred to the pristine waters of the Sounds, where they are farmed in a completely natural environment.

Because the sun, wind and tides clean the farms, there is no need for the antibiotics, vaccines and chemicals commonly used overseas.

Salmon is a relatively economical source of top-quality protein and vitamins and is an excellent source of omega-3, linked to protection against heart disease and certain cancers, alleviation of arthritic pain, and boosting of the immune system. But best of all its taste and versatility makes salmon a favourite of home cooks.

Do not overcook this gourmet delight – it is ready to eat when the flesh turns opaque.

Chopstix Salmon

¼ cup each: rice wine vinegar, lemon juice

1 tablespoon each: finely grated root ginger, grated palm sugar, fish sauce

400g Regal Salmon Fillet

16-20 small rocket leaves

Combine the rice wine vinegar, lemon juice, ginger, palm sugar and fish sauce.

Cut the salmon into 3cm cubes. Place in a glass or ceramic bowl and add the combined ingredients. Mix well. Cover and marinate for about 8 hours, stirring occasionally, until the salmon takes on a 'cooked' appearance.

Place each salmon cube between disposable chopsticks together with a small rocket leaf.

Bring the marinade mixture to the boil and simmer for 1 minute. Cool and serve as a dipping sauce. **SERVES 8-10 AS AN APPETISER.**

WINE MATCH

The fresh, zesty flavours of lemon juice and ginger together with the gorgeous texture of this marinated salmon make the Elstree bubbles the perfect match. The creaminess of the wine provides a lovely contrast to the vibrant flavours of the dish, while the acidity in both is complementary.

Highfield Elstree Marlborough Cuvée Brut

This wine is made employing the traditional two fermentations – the first is 50% in French oak and 50% in stainless steel and the second is in the bottle. The resulting wine has a lovely creamy texture as the acidity has softened during its maturation, yet the fruit remains lively and refreshing.

Maple-glazed Salmon with Summer Salsa

4 x 175g Regal Salmon Steaks

1 tablespoon each: maple syrup, kecap manis, marmalade, lemon juice

1 clove garlic, crushed

1 teaspoon finely grated root ginger

Summer Salsa

1 medium ripe tomato, diced

½ avocado, stoned, peeled and diced

½ teaspoon chopped chilli

2 each: ripe nectarines, peaches, stoned and diced

1 teaspoon sugar

Using tweezers, remove as many pin bones from the steaks as possible.

Combine the maple syrup, kecap manis, marmalade, lemon juice, garlic and ginger in a bowl. Place the salmon in a single layer in a dish. Spoon the marinade over the top. Cover and refrigerate for 1-24 hours.

To prepare the salsa, mix all the ingredients in a small bowl.

Grill the salmon for about 4-6 minutes each side, depending on the thickness. Serve with the salsa. **SERVES 4.**

WINE MATCH

The tropical nature of the salsa is great with a tropical style of Sauvignon Blanc such as the Highfield, and the fresh acidity in the wine balances the rich texture and sweetness of the salmon.

Highfield Marlborough Sauvignon Blanc

Shows plenty of tropical fruit on the nose such as mango, passion fruit and pineapple and these are repeated on the palate. A wine that is ideal on its own or with a range of seafood dishes or salads.

AL SOPER, WINEMAKER, HIGHFIELD ESTATE

"One of the best things about Marlborough is the way the local wild food complements the local wines. It's great that we can visit the coast to gather paua or the Sounds to get mussels or scallops, or dive for crayfish. And because you can be eating your bounty within a couple of hours, nothing compares to enjoying mussels and Sauvignon Blanc, scallops and Chardonnay or sparkling wine and oysters. If you're into hunting, the nearby mountain ranges offer wild deer, pigs and goat. That's far too energetic for me. I'm more than happy to swap Pinot Noir for venison or boar when my mates bring some down from the hills."

11

Pinot Noir-poached Salmon

400g Regal Salmon Fillet or
  2 Regal Salmon Steaks,
  about 2.5cm thick

juice ½ lemon

flaky salt and freshly ground
  black pepper to taste

¾ cup Pinot Noir

¼ cup water

25g butter

Wash the salmon and pat dry. Squeeze the lemon juice over the top and season.

Simmer the wine and water in a frying pan about 5cm deep. Reduce the heat to low. Add the salmon in a single layer. Cover and poach (skin-side down if using the fillet) for about 5-8 minutes, depending on thickness, until just cooked. Remember – the salmon continues to cook after it is removed from the heat. Carefully transfer the salmon to a platter. Cover and keep warm.

Boil the liquid until reduced to about a ⅓ of a cup.

Remove from the heat. Whisk in the butter. Pour the sauce over the salmon just before serving. **SERVES 2.**

WINE MATCH

This fish just melts in the mouth and of course, having been poached in Pinot Noir, the pairing with this Highfield wine works very well. A deliciously different dish.

Highfield Pinot Noir

Plum and berry fruit on the nose together with hints of mocha. The palate is smooth and balanced with lovely ripe cherry flavours and a long finish with a hint of savouriness.

New Zealand King Salmon produces 80 per cent of New Zealand's and 40 per cent of the world's farmed Pacific King (or Chinook) salmon. The New Zealand King Salmon Company Limited was formed in 1996 with the privatisation and merger of New Zealand's two largest salmon companies, Southern Ocean Seafood Ltd and Regal Salmon Ltd.

Marlborough **Regal Salmon** is available from supermarkets and fish shops throughout the country in a wide variety of cuts and styles, including whole fresh and frozen salmon, fresh chilled fillets and steaks, salmon kebabs and smoked salmon. Rich red-orange Regal Salmon is enjoyed for its exceptional flavour, its versatility and ease of use.

Highfield Estate

As well as a range of five impressive wines, Highfield Estate is perhaps best known locally for its unique, high-profile headquarters located high in the vineyards above Brookby Road. Designed by Sir Michael Fowler, the building is based on a Tuscan fortress, complete with a tower and terracotta roof tiles.

Nestling inside this impressive structure is Highfield's award-winning cellar door and restaurant. The restaurant showcases local produce and is a very popular destination for locals and visitors alike.

The company's flagship wine is Elstree Cuvée Brut, a vintage specific Méthode Traditionelle created in conjunction with Michel Drappier of the family-owned Champagne house, Drappier et Fils.

Each of the company's five labels is made to the highest possible standard, optimising the characters of each grape variety. The result is rich, full-bodied, flavoursome wines. The Chardonnay is barrel-fermented and undergoes 100% malolactic fermentation (converting the sharper malic acid to creamy lactic acid) to give a big, rich, almost caramel character while the Riesling is of medium style packed with floral notes such as citrus blossom and jasmine. The Sauvignon Blanc offers a more tropical representation of this popular grape variety while the Pinot Noir is handcrafted using open-top fermenters and hand-plunging followed by almost a year in French oak barrels.

Salmon Success

When most people think of Marlborough they think of the spectacular Sounds and, of course fine wines, particularly Sauvignon Blanc – arguably the world's best. Food lovers would also claim another world-beater for the region – Pacific King salmon.

The first attempts to introduce King salmon, a native of the northern Pacific, to South Island rivers as a game fish were made in the 19th century. It was a case of 'the one that got away' – multiplied by several millions. The young salmon fry swam happily off into the cool currents never to be seen again. Success finally came when salmon bred from eggs imported from California were released into the headwaters of the Waitaki, Rangitata, Rakaia and Waimakariri rivers.

The fighting game fish became a farmed favourite in 1983 with the establishment of New Zealand's first sea cage salmon farm in Stewart Island waters. Over the years fish farming has become a highly efficient, environment-friendly industry helping to ease the pressure on wild fish, which are being exploited beyond sustainable limits. Traditional fishing methods can not only dangerously deplete stocks of target species but also kill many other species of fish along with birds and mammals. Aquaculture offers a sustainable supply of healthy fish without harming other wildlife.

Nestling in the pristine Marlborough Sounds in carefully chosen remote locations where tides flush water in from the deep Cook Strait trough are the New Zealand King Salmon Company farms that produce 80 per cent of New Zealand's – and 40 per cent of the world's – Pacific King Salmon. The temperature and purity of the water are critical and because the sun, wind and tides clean the farms there is no requirement for the antibiotics, vaccines and chemicals commonly employed by overseas producers. Strict monitoring ensures that there is an absence of the diseases that cause problems in the northern hemisphere.

Replicating a natural lifestyle fit for a king is essential. At the hatcheries in Golden Bay, Canterbury and Marlborough, eggs are collected and fertilized under a sophisticated brood stock and family selection programme ensuring regal results.

Several months later, at a time when they would normally be migrating to the ocean, the smolt (young salmon) are transferred to the sea cages in the Marlborough Sounds where they are left to grow for up to 18 months. As no growth hormones are used the all-natural result is a healthy, gourmet delight.

Pacific King salmon has the highest natural oil content of all salmon – a 150-gram portion provides the complete daily requirement of omega-3, which is linked to protection against heart disease, certain cancers, alleviation of arthritic pain and boosting of the immune system.

Pacific King salmon in a variety of sizes – 2 to 5 kilograms plus – are harvested every week of the year. Highly efficient processing operations mean that customers anywhere in New Zealand can be enjoying a taste of Marlborough within 24 hours of harvesting. For international customers it is 48-60 hours.

The ready availability of the king of salmon means that it is no longer considered to be a special treat. The price – about the same as snapper – puts this tantalizing entertainer's delight on the menu of every home cook.

Pacific King is the only salmon species farmed in sea cages in New Zealand. As one of the world's major suppliers, New Zealand is setting a healthy pace in expanding the market and offering appetizing alternatives to fish caught by traditional methods.

To paraphrase Lewis Carroll (*Alice's Adventures In Wonderland*)

"Will you walk a little faster?" said a 'wild fish' to a snail,

"There's a King salmon right behind us, and he's treading on my tail."

SAFFRON

Saffron – one of the most prized and expensive spices in the world – thrives in the hot, dry Marlborough climate. In autumn, mauve crocus flowers, encasing bright red stigmas (the saffron), spike through the soil.

Each morning, the flowers are picked by hand before the warmth of the sun opens the petals to expose the stigmas, which cannot be contaminated in any way. Even pollen from the stamen will affect the quality.

Once picked, nimble fingers separate the stigmas cleanly and uniformly from the flower. The stigmas are dried quickly to capture aroma, taste and colour then stored in cool, dry darkness until packed for sale.

Each blossom has just three stigmas. It is estimated that about 75,000 blossoms are necessary to yield 500g of saffron. Luckily, a little goes a long way.

Scallops with Saffron

¾ cup each: fish stock, Sauvignon Blanc

¼ teaspoon Gourmet Gold Saffron threads

1 tablespoon olive oil

1 small shallot, finely diced

1 bunch fresh herbs

salt and pepper to taste

16 scallops

2 tablespoons finely chopped parsley

Bring the stock and wine to the boil. Add the saffron and stand for at least 5 minutes.

Heat the oil in a non-stick pan and sauté the shallot, until softened. Add the stock mixture and herbs. Boil, until reduced by half. Season. Remove the bunch of herbs.

Add the scallops to the sauce and poach until just warm, turning them several times during cooking. Add the chopped parsley.

Excellent served with crusty bread and a crisp salad on the side. **SERVES 2 AS A LIGHT MEAL.**

WINE MATCH

The earthy, warm and unusual flavour of saffron works very well with the herbaceous qualities of Seresin Sauvignon Blanc while the soft texture of the scallops also makes for a good match.

Seresin Sauvignon Blanc

This wine is a full-flavoured example of the region's most popular variety. A balanced offering of ripe passionfruit together with freshly-picked summer herbs, a citrus acidity and slightly creamy mouth-feel.

Saffron Panna Cotta

2 teaspoons powdered
  gelatine
2 tablespoons water
1¼ cups cream
¾ cup milk
2 tablespoons sugar
¼ teaspoon Gourmet Gold
  Saffron threads
1 teaspoon vanilla essence
¼ teaspoon canola oil

Soften the gelatine in the water for 5 minutes.

Place the cream, milk, sugar, saffron and vanilla essence in a saucepan and bring to the boil. Whisk the gelatine into the hot milk mixture. Remove from the heat and cool.

Take six small moulds and lightly brush with the oil. This makes the panna cotta easier to remove.

Carefully skim off any air bubbles from the top of the panna cotta mixture. Pour evenly into the moulds and refrigerate, until set.

To remove from the mould, tip each panna cotta on its side and run a small knife around the top edge of the mould. Tip the panna cotta into six serving dishes.

Garnish with fruit (eg poached peaches) and a little fruit juice or liqueur. **SERVES 6**.

WINE MATCH

It is unusual to match Chardonnay with a sweet dish, but the toasty, spicy nature of the saffron and the wine's intense flavours and oak go very well together, as do the creamy texture of both.

Seresin Reserve Chardonnay

This is a powerful yet elegant expression of Chardonnay at its best. Rich and flavoursome yet offers an underlying mineral element together with the nutty, toasty oak. This wine has ripe citrus and melon flavours that last forever.

CLIVE DOUGALL, WINEMAKER, SERESIN ESTATE

"What I love about Marlborough is getting out on my boat for a dive to collect some scallops or crayfish. Or fish for some of the many species that inhabit the area. It's an amazing feeling to be able to spend the day on the water in some of the most beautiful spots in the world, and then come home with some of the best and freshest seafood you could wish for. Naturally I like to match the seafood with some of our wines and olive oils. My favourite is fresh scallops, pan-fried in a little of our lemon-infused olive oil matched with a glass of our Reserve Chardonnay."

Paella with Saffron & Chorizo

3 cups good fish stock

½ teaspoon Gourmet Gold Saffron threads

1 each: large green pepper (capsicum), onion

1 tablespoon each: olive oil, chopped garlic

1½ cups long grain rice

2 large tomatoes, diced

2 spicy chorizo sausages, sliced

300g cooked mussels in the half-shell

freshly ground salt and pepper to taste

Bring the stock to the boil. Combine the saffron with a ¼ cup of the stock. Stand for a few minutes to infuse.

Halve, seed and dice the pepper. Dice the onion.

Heat the oil in a large, non-stick frying pan. Add the pepper, onion and garlic and cook until soft. Sprinkle the rice into the pan and stir-fry for 1 minute.

Add the remainder of the boiling stock together with the tomatoes and saffron mixture. Bring to the boil then reduce the heat. Cover and cook, without stirring, for about 12 minutes, until the rice has absorbed most of the stock.

Add the chorizo and mussels to the rice and season. Cover and steam for about 5 minutes, until heated through.

SERVES 4.

WINE MATCH

This multi-flavoured dish needs a wine with plenty of flavour, but not so much as to overpower. Seresin Pinot Noir is ideal with its lifted spicy characters and ripe forest-floor fruit.

Seresin Leah Pinot Noir

This is a sumptuous Pinot Noir with mouth-coating richness and great depth of flavour and texture due to being unfiltered. The ripe fruit is reminiscent of cherries, plums and blackberries while the finish is long and succulent with mocha and spice overtones.

Gourmet Gold Saffron is tested annually against ISO standards and has always rated Category 1. In addition to pure saffron threads, Gourmet Gold also produces Saffron Aioli and a Lime & Saffron Marmalade – ideal for those with a passion for the unique. Gourmet Gold Saffron can be ordered online or purchased at the Marlborough Farmers' Market.

Owners Jill and Louise, suggest that a ½ gram sachet of Gourmet Gold Saffron threads equates to 4 teaspoons of threads or 8 pinches of threads. It provides enough saffron to colour and flavour two to four meals for six people. Experiment with a little saffron and increase it slowly to suit your taste.

Seresin Estate

Renowned film-maker, Michael Seresin, bought 167 acres of land in the Wairau Valley in 1992 and planted Sauvignon Blanc, Chardonnay, Riesling, Pinot Gris and Pinot Noir. The wines from the first vintage in 1996 were made in the estate's brand new, gravity-fed winery ensuring minimal handling of the fruit in a pristine environment.

Everything about Seresin Estate has a natural, understated and authentic feel about it. The use of the simple handprint as their company symbol, the biodynamic vineyards and use of natural yeasts for fermentation – all contribute to the production of premium wine using traditional, artisan winemaking methods.

During the building of the winery everyone that contributed to its construction was asked to leave their handprint on the walls as an acknowledgement of the importance of the hand as man's first signature, dating back as far as 30,000 years ago, 'This is my mark. This is my work.'

The hand on the Seresin wine label identifies the company in a very simple and effective way and it has justifiably become one of the most easily recognised and coveted New Zealand wine brands.

STONE FRUIT

Delicious, versatile and affordable, nectarines, peaches, apricots and plums are the true essence of summer – the tastes that linger. Savouring tree-ripened Marlborough delights is pure joy.

There are two types of nectarines available – the traditional golden-fleshed and the newer, white-fleshed variety. The latter are excellent in salads. Choose plump, well-coloured (orange-yellow to red skinned) nectarines with a slight softening at the point and along the suture. If necessary, soften at room temperature until ripe, then refrigerate.

Stone fruit are as versatile as they are colourful. Slice some over your muesli or porridge; top pikelets or scones with sliced fruit and whipped cream; combine with salad greens, ham and balsamic dressing for a light lunch; slice and serve with cheese on crackers with five o'clock drinks; roast in a little butter and serve with meat; or top with your favourite crumble mix, bake and serve hot for dessert.

Spiced Oven-roasted Plums

spray oil
8 plums, halved and stoned
½ cup orange juice
2 tablespoons brown sugar
½ teaspoon ground cinnamon
⅛ teaspoon each: ground nutmeg, cumin, cardamom

Preheat the oven to 200°C. Spray a shallow baking dish with oil.

Place the plums, cut-side up, in a single layer in the baking dish.

Combine the orange juice, brown sugar, cinnamon, nutmeg, cumin, and cardamom in a bowl. Drizzle over the plums.

Bake for about 20 minutes, or until the plums are hot and the sauce is bubbly. Excellent served with beef, pork or lamb. **SERVES 4.**

WINE MATCH

Served with red meat, these oven-roasted plums offer a sweet yet slightly tart accompaniment and taste delicious with this fruit-driven style of Spy Valley Pinot Noir.

Spy Valley Pinot Noir

A medium-bodied Pinot with ripe, upfront flavours of raspberry, cherry and plum together with some toasted spice. A very approachable style but with a good backbone giving it further potential as it matures in the bottle.

Marinated Char-grilled Peaches

3-4 peaches
½ cup orange juice
¼ cup honey liqueur
2 star anise
2 tablespoons each: sugar, melted butter

Halve and stone the peaches.
   Combine the orange juice, honey liqueur, star anise and sugar and bring to the boil.
   Place the peaches on a grilling rack or ridged frying pan. Brush with the orange mixture.
   Grill until slightly softened, turn and brush with the butter. Continue cooking for 1-2 minutes.
   Great served with mascarpone or whipped cream.
SERVES 4-6.

WINE MATCH

The peach flavours here are delicious with this aromatic, enticing Spy Valley wine. Neither is too sweet and the added hint of toastiness from grilling the fruit is a lovely unexpected addition.

Spy Valley Gewurztraminer

Full-flavoured with a wonderful balance of sweetness, acidity and texture, this is the ideal wine for Gewurz lovers! Packed with exotic fruit flavours this slightly sweet style is perfect with many dishes that contain an element of sweetness, such as Thai food.

PAUL BOURGEOIS, CHIEF WINEMAKER, SPY VALLEY

"For me the best thing about Marlborough food and wine is the freshness and choice available between vibrant bold flavours or more subtle complex ones. I love the wildlife around Marlborough especially when it is on a plate. Fresh sea-run brown trout, caught from the Wairau River, covered in sea salt and brown sugar and then quickly hot-smoked is pretty hard to beat. The surprisingly subtle but instantly gratifying taste of whitebait from the lower Opawa River, big fat succulent scallops from Queen Charlotte Sound, dripping with butter, freshly speared butterfish (the name says it all) or blue cod. Last but not least, wild pork bacon on warm fresh crusty bread."

Nectarine & Mozzarella Salad

200g fresh mozzarella cheese, sliced into thick strips

2 tablespoons balsamic vinegar

4 tablespoons extra virgin olive oil

4 nectarines, halved and stoned

1 tablespoon lemon juice

4 cups small rocket leaves

freshly ground black pepper to taste

Place the mozzarella in a bowl. Whisk the vinegar and olive oil and drizzle over the cheese. Marinate for 1-2 hours.

Cut each halved nectarine in half. Brush the cut side of the nectarines with a little lemon juice.

Place the rocket in the centre of four dinner plates. Top with the cheese.

Arrange the nectarines on top. Sprinkle with a little of the dressing (marinade). Sprinkle with generous amounts of freshly ground black pepper. Serve immediately. **SERVES 4 AS A STARTER.**

WINE MATCH

The lovely fresh flavours of this dish are a cinch with this fragrant Spy Valley Riesling and its hint of sweetness. The creamy cheese and the nectarine make an appealing contrast while the wine brings the flavours together.

Spy Valley Riesling

Aromatic with floral and citrus characters, this mouth-watering Riesling offers ripe and succulent fruit flavours together with a fresh acidity making it a perfectly balanced wine.

When in season, (December through February) two of the best places to purchase Marlborough stone fruit is either at: the **Farmers' Market** held every Sunday morning at the AMP Showgrounds. October through to May, from 9am until noon; or at the **Redwoodtown Market** on Alabama road on Saturday mornings.

Local stone fruit is used to make liqueurs and preserves and these are also often available at the markets.

Spy Valley

This innovative producer is owned by the Johnson family and produced its first wines in 2000. Named after the nearby communications monitoring station with its two huge white domes, Spy Valley makes wine from the ten grape varieties grown on its 380-acre estate in Marlborough's Waihopai Valley.

The state-of-the-art winery was built in stages between 2003 and 2007 and is perfectly tailored to produce great wine. Designed in sympathy with its surroundings, it has been awarded the New Zealand Institute of Architects Supreme Commercial Award and in addition, the landscaping received the Marlborough Environment Award.

Predominantly known for its aromatic wines such as Gewuztraminer, Riesling and Pinot Gris, the company's complete range has won numerous wine show awards and accolades from some of the world's most influential wine publications.

Now exporting to 26 markets worldwide, Spy Valley excels at taking its unique story to the wine consumer. From the labels to the web site, the designer clothing to the cellar door, everything about Spy Valley is consistent and of an exceptionally high quality.

WILD GAME

Marlborough is rabbit country. Local farmers and grape growers are only too pleased to see rabbit, regarded as a pest, served out of a saucepan rather than nibbling at their crops. As with most game, rabbit is a lean meat and is best when casseroled, or regularly basted if being roasted.

Wild pork is another Marlborough game delight. With many locals heading off to the bush-clad Richmond Range each weekend, wild pigs are often seen tied to the back of a ute on their way to the butcher.

Wild pork has a unique flavour that is still definitely 'pork', but with a stronger taste. It is delicious as a roast leg or casseroled.

A small team of hunters who have their licences renewed annually, work together with landowners to ensure the environment is unharmed.

Rabbit with Tomato & Herbs

1kg Premium Game Rabbit portions

¼ cup flour

salt and freshly ground black pepper to taste

2 tablespoons olive oil

2 rashers wild pork bacon, chopped

2½ cups good tomato-based pasta sauce

1 cup Sauvignon Blanc

1 bunch fresh herbs eg bay leaf, thyme, rosemary, basil

Dredge the rabbit portions in the combined flour, salt and pepper. Shake off any excess.

Heat the oil in a heavy pan and sauté the rabbit in batches, until well coloured. Add the bacon and sauté, until coloured. Pour in the pasta sauce and wine. Add the herbs and bring to the boil. Cover and simmer on low heat for 1½ - 2 hours, until cooked. Alternatively, cook in a slow cooker on low for 8 hours or a 170°C oven for 2 hours.

Excellent served with spiral pasta or penne. **SERVES 4-6**.

WINE MATCH

Sauvignon Blanc works admirably with tomato-based sauces and with the added herbs of this dish it is ideal. The lovely fleshy texture of this full-flavoured Saint Clair Sauvignon is great with the lean rabbit too.

Saint Clair Pioneer Block 3 Sauvignon Blanc

This is a big, powerful expression of Sauvignon Blanc offering lots of freshly chopped green herbs and underlying guava and passionfruit. Quite fleshy on the palate with significant length.

Wild Pork & Red Wine

1kg cubed Premium Game
Wild Pork

2 cups good red wine

4 rashers Premium Game
Wild Pork Bacon,
chopped

1-2 tablespoons olive oil

1 large onion, diced

4 tablespoons flour

freshly ground salt and
pepper to taste

1 bouquet garni (bunch of
fresh herbs)

Place the pork in a bowl and add the wine. Mix well, cover and refrigerate for several hours. Drain, reserving the wine. Pat the meat dry. Preheat the oven to 160°C.

Sauté the bacon in the oil in a frying pan, until crisp. Add the onion and sauté for 2 minutes. Place in a casserole.

Sprinkle the pork with the flour and sauté in batches in the pan, until coloured. Place in the casserole with the seasonings and herbs. Add the red wine to the frying pan and bring to the boil, scraping any burnt pieces from the pan. Pour into the casserole.

Cover and cook in the oven for 2 hours, until tender. May be served garnished with herbs. **SERVES 4-6**.

WINE MATCH

Saint Clair Pinot Noir is a great partner for game as the fruit flavours work very well to balanced the savoury, gamey flavours of the dish and the naturally firm acidity in Pinot cuts through any richness.

Saint Clair Marlborough Pinot Noir

This ripe, cherry-berry style of Pinot is a delight. Medium-bodied and fresh with lots of juicy berry fruit and a fine, balancing acidity along with gentle tannin. An easy style to enjoy.

HAMISH CLARK, SENIOR WINEMAKER, SAINT CLAIR FAMILY ESTATE

"I love the fact that in Marlborough, everything is on the doorstep. For the hunter-gatherer, treats are aplenty from land, sea and air and all readily available to those willing to spend a little time to gather them. Scallops, freshly shucked and poached in a little clarified butter, a few shavings of ginger and a splash of Riesling; mussels, paua, crayfish, fresh fish, hare, manuka-smoked wild bacon, wild duck – the list goes on. We produce and possess some of the finest things to indulge the taste buds and stimulate the mind and body, right here. That for me is the beauty of living in Marlborough."

Wild Goat Curry

2-3 tablespoons garlic-infused rice bran oil

2 large onions, sliced

1 tablespoon curry powder

2 tablespoons flour

1 kg diced Premium Game Wild Goat Meat

2 teaspoons finely grated root ginger

freshly ground black pepper to taste

pinch ground cloves

1 apple, cored and diced

2 tablespoons tomato paste

400ml can coconut milk

Preheat the oven to 160 °C.

Heat a little oil in a heavy saucepan and sauté the onions, until softened.

Combine the curry powder and flour. Dust the goat with the flour mixture to coat well. Add to the saucepan and stir until lightly browned. Season with the ginger, pepper and ground cloves. Add the apple, tomato paste and coconut milk. Stir well. Cover and cook in the oven for 1½ hours or until tender.

Great served on rice. **SERVES 4**.

WINE MATCH

This dish with its coconut and spices is ideal with this full-flavoured Saint Clair Chardonnay. The creamy characters of both work well together.

Saint Clair Omaka Reserve Chardonnay

A delicious, rich and toasty Chardonnay with a combination of ripe stone fruit, mealy yeast characters and lots of toasted oak. Full-bodied, this is a very satisfying and rich style of wine.

The leading supplier of local wild game is **Premium Game**, located just south of Blenheim at the Riverlands Estate. New Zealand has a wide range of introduced game animals that can be hunted, which are processed by Premium Game for the New Zealand domestic market.

Premium Game supplies a variety of high-quality wild game meats, including wild venison, pork, goat, tahr, hare, rabbit and wallaby. By controlling introduced game species, New Zealand's high country environment is improved. Premium Game's operation has no negative effect on the environment.

Saint Clair Family Estate

From among the first of Marlborough's grape growers back in 1978 to one of today's most dynamic and prolific wine producers, Neal and Judy Ibbotson's Saint Clair label has accomplished a considerable amount. Now exporting to 55 markets around the world, the portfolio of some 40 wines can be found in some of the world's most prestigious restaurants and residences – even the luxurious Emirates Palace in Abu Dhabi.

The Saint Clair name has a strong historical link with Marlborough as it relates to pioneer James Sinclair who owned the original vineyard land and was closely associated with the development of Blenheim, building some of the town's first homes. Today, the company is very much a family estate with the Ibbotson children, Tony, Sarina and Julie all involved.

For lovers of Sauvignon Blanc, this is perhaps where the company excels, with no less than a dozen different Sauvignon Blanc wines included in the Saint Clair range. Saint Clair's Wairau Reserve is New Zealand's most awarded Sauvignon Blanc and has won an outstanding 30 trophies at local and international wine shows since 2001. These wines are made from exceptional small parcels of fruit chosen by Saint Clair's winemakers from selected specialist vineyard sites that have been identified as having a unique terroir in the Marlborough region.

SCALLOPS

One of the most delightful aspects of being a Marlburian is having friends who share their local gourmet delights with you. And scallops are always a treat.

Simply sautéed in a little butter or olive oil, seasoned and cooked on the barbecue is a great way to serve scallops whether it be at home or at the beach. Just remember to sauté scallops on medium heat and not to over-cook them. The scallop meat will turn opaque as it is heated and is best served medium-rare.

Try scallops poached in a little Marlborough Riesling or Sauvignon Blanc then skewered along with a cube of local rockmelon; or serve with a salsa prepared with diced peaches or nectarines, diced chilli and chopped coriander leaves.

Marinated Scallops

24 scallops

1/3 cup lemon juice

1 small green pepper (capsicum), seeded and diced

1 kaffir lime leaf, finely julienned

2 tablespoons extra virgin olive oil

flaky salt and freshly ground black pepper to taste

Halve any large scallops, if preferred. Place in a bowl with the lemon juice. Cover and marinate for 4-6 hours or overnight, turning occasionally. Drain.

Combine the diced pepper, kaffir lime leaf and oil. Mix well then season. Combine with the scallops.

Place in individual serving dishes. **SERVES 4 AS A STARTER.**

WINE MATCH

Tailor-made for Lawson's Sauvignon Blanc, the fresh flavours of the zesty lemon, kaffir lime and green capsicum together with the succulent scallops is just mouth-watering. Uplifting and vibrant.

Lawson's Dry Hills Sauvignon Blanc

This is a lovely fleshy style of Sauvignon Blanc with an attractive balance of fresh garden herbs and ripe, juicy passion fruit. A fresh acidity and gentle mineral tone give the wine both backbone and length.

Scallops, Peaches & Bacon

24 scallops

salt and pepper to taste

2-3 ripe but firm peaches, stoned and peeled

4 rashers streaky rindless bacon

3-4 tablespoons olive oil

Drain the scallops and pat dry. Season.

Slice the peaches. Cut the bacon into strips long enough to wrap a slice of peach and a scallop together. Thread onto little skewers or cocktail sticks. Brush with oil.

Place under a preheated grill for about 5 minutes, turning occasionally. **SERVES 6 AS AN APPETISER.**

WINE MATCH

The sweet and savoury mix of flavours of these skewers is perfect for Lawson's Gewurztraminer as the fruity richness of the wine matches the sweet peach and savoury bacon, while the scallop flavours are nestled between the two.

Lawson's Dry Hills Gewurztraminer

Another of the region's most heralded wines; this Gewurztraminer is one in a long line of award winners for this winery. Richly aromatic and flavoured with spice, Turkish delight and white flowers and offering a long, sumptuous finish.

MARCUS WRIGHT, WINEMAKER, LAWSON'S DRY HILLS

"We really are spoilt for food, wine and scenery here in Marlborough. Picnicking with the family on a secluded beach in the Sounds or a long Sunday lunch at home with friends are real pleasures. The best lunch is the culmination of a diving trip and a visit to the Farmers' Market. Scallops are easily gathered and simply prepared with a little lemon-infused olive oil and garlic then tossed on the barbecue and served with artisan breads, terrines and fresh tomatoes. Summer and fresh seafood is the best match for Lawson's Dry Hills Sauvignon Blanc. I get through a bit over the course of the summer as you can imagine!"

Curry-crusted Scallops

Pea Purée

250g peas

¼ cup water

1 tablespoon butter-infused rice bran oil

1 large shallot, diced

1 tablespoon lime juice

flaky salt to taste

Scallops

2 teaspoons curry powder

2 tablespoons flour

flaky salt and pepper to taste

24 scallops

2 tablespoons butter-infused rice bran oil

1 large lime, quartered

Simmer the peas in the water for about 3 minutes or until cooked. Do not drain. Purée together with the cooking water, rice bran oil, shallot, lime juice and salt.

Combine the curry powder, flour and seasonings and spread on a plate. Pat the scallops dry. Toss in the curry mixture.

Heat the oil in a large non-stick frying pan over medium-high heat, until hot. Sauté the scallops, turning once, until browned and just cooked through, about 4 minutes.

Reheat the purée and place in the centre of four entrée-sized plates. Top with the scallops. Serve with wedges of lime on the side. **SERVES 4**.

WINE MATCH

The slightly spicy flavour of the curried scallops and the lovely spicy, ripe fruit in this Lawson's Riesling are a treat while the fresh flavours of the pea purée are great with the zesty, fresh acidity in the wine.

Lawson's Dry Hills Riesling

This is a lovely example of good Marlborough Riesling. Lime and honey – though this is a dry wine – give way to lingering white peach flavours and the acidity chases the ripe fruits to ensure a zesty, refreshing glass of wine.

The scallop is a popular bivalve mollusc with two beautiful fan-shaped shells that are often used as serving dishes. The entire scallop including the roe is edible. The local species, 'pecten novaezealandie', is peculiar to New Zealand although similar species occur elsewhere.

The scallop catch is subject to restricted sizes, seasons and quota and the Marlborough season runs from mid-July until mid-February. The legal bag limit for scallops is 50 per fisher per day. In addition, divers are entitled to take an extra daily bag for each of up to two 'safety' people on-board a boat.

Lawson's Dry Hills

Ross and Barbara had been growing Gewurztraminer grapes for other wine companies on their Alabama Road site since 1980 before starting their own label in 1992. With Gewurztraminer and other aromatics such as Pinot Gris their forte, the company quickly developed into one of the most successful in Marlborough and now exports to numerous markets worldwide.

Prior to making wine, Barbara was a hospital theatre nurse while Ross took on various jobs including musterer, shearer, swimming pool builder and opossum hunter. Ross has never been afraid to turn his hand to anything and make it work, something he proved yet again with the introduction of the New Zealand Screwcap Wine Seal Initiative which he helped found in 2001 with the primary purpose of facilitating the use of screwcap wine seals on New Zealand's premium quality wines.

Another member of the Lawson's team is Tomi – a rather spherical golden Labrador who signals the start of vintage each year with her enthusiastic chomping of the ripe grapes!

Lawson's Dry Hills range of wines include Sauvignon Blanc, Chardonnay, Riesling, Gewurztraminer, Pinot Gris and Pinot Noir, all sourced from Marlborough's Wairau, Waihopai, Omaka and Brancott valleys.

GARLIC & SHALLOTS

Those with a taste for tall tales will know that garlic wards off vampires. If true, then the fleshy, flavoursome Marlborough garlic would be the ultimate defence.

The local garlic is generally much more tasty than that of imported varieties. One clove has as much flavour as three of the imports. This is because of the ideal growing conditions in Marlborough – garlic loves frosts and hot summers – plus the fact that it does not need to be cool-stored which dehydrates the bulbs.

Shallots, like garlic, belong to the lily family. They are favoured for their mild, sweet flavour and can be used in the same manner as onions. The bulbs generally break into two – use both in robust dishes or one in more delicate dishes.

Garlic Mushrooms

4 cloves NZ Garlic, crushed

¼ cup butter-infused rice bran oil

8 large portabello mushrooms

4 anchovies, drained and chopped

1 tablespoon capers, rinsed, drained and chopped

½ cup finely chopped parsley

2 tablespoons each: finely chopped almonds, Pinot Noir

freshly ground black pepper to taste

Combine half the garlic with 3 tablespoons of the oil. Brush over the mushrooms. Grill or barbecue, until tender.

Combine the remaining garlic with the anchovies, capers, parsley, almonds, wine, remaining oil and black pepper. Spoon the mixture onto the mushrooms.

Great served with lightly grilled ciabatta. **SERVES 4 AS A STARTER.**

WINE MATCH

The earthy taste of mushrooms is ideal with Lake Chalice Pinot Noir. The addition of garlic enhances the wine's fruit characters, while the acidity keeps it all from being too rich.

Lake Chalice Pinot Noir

Classic aromas of red fruits with some rich savoury undertones of spicy oak lead to a medium-bodied wine with an appealing soft palate. Gentle tannins and well-balanced acidity support the cherry fruit flavours.

Chicken with Caramelised Shallots

4 rashers rindless bacon, thinly sliced

8 chicken thigh cutlets

freshly ground black pepper to taste

1 tablespoon olive oil

400g NZ Shallots, thinly sliced

12 cloves NZ Garlic

1 cup chicken stock

¼ cup balsamic vinegar

Stir the bacon on low heat in a large, heavy saucepan, until crisp. Drain on paper towels. Reserve the bacon fat.

Pat the chicken dry and season. Quickly brown in batches in the bacon fat. Drain on paper towels.

Add the oil and shallots to the pan. Cover and cook on medium-low, until pale golden, about 10 minutes. Uncover. Continue cooking until deep golden, about 10 minutes. Add the garlic and stock. Boil for 1 minute.

Return the chicken to the saucepan. Cover and simmer until the chicken is cooked and the garlic is tender, 30-40 minutes.

Transfer the chicken to a serving dish and keep warm. Add the balsamic vinegar to the sauce. Simmer, mashing the garlic with the back of a spoon. When thickened, pour over the chicken. Top with the bacon. **SERVES 4**.

WINE MATCH

Both the wine and the dish are ostensibly dry in flavour but both have a hint of sweetness, the Lake Chalice with its touch of residual sugar and the caramelised shallots in the dish.

Lake Chalice Pinot Gris

Citrus blossom and white peach on the nose are also reflected on the palate. This off-dry style of Pinot Gris has a refreshing mineral undertone along with a lovely balanced acidity. A gentle style that is easy to enjoy.

CHRIS GAMBITSIS, DIRECTOR, LAKE CHALICE

"Second Saturday in February: hot days, cool nights. I've invited a few close, personal friends (well, more than a few) to celebrate Marlborough Wine Festival weekend. A little jaded from long hours behind the bar and the grill, our guests fly in from New Zealand's best restaurants. They are a little thirsty, a little hungry and ready to party. Over the weekend we make new friends and renew old friendships over seared prawns, mussels – out comes the Sauvignon Blanc and the Riesling. Barbecue-baked whole beef fillet and later, lamb backstraps, bring on the Pinot Noir and Merlot! Tasty food, great wine and good friends. Bring it on."

Pumpkin Risotto

2 large NZ Shallots, finely chopped

2 tablespoons olive oil

1½ cups arborio rice

1 glass Chardonnay

2 cloves NZ Garlic, crushed

200g peeled and seeded pumpkin, diced

7-8 cups low-salt chicken or vegetable stock

50g each: grated Parmesan cheese, unsalted butter

¼ cup each: chopped flat-leaf parsley, cream (optional)

Fry the shallots in 1 tablespoon of the oil in a large saucepan. Add the rice and toast it – stirring – for 4-5 minutes. Add the wine and garlic and simmer, until evaporated.

Place the remaining oil and the pumpkin in another pan. Stir well. Cover and cook for about 10 minutes, stirring occasionally.

Bring the stock to the boil. Add enough stock to just cover the rice. Simmer, stirring constantly until the rice has absorbed the liquid. Keep stirring in the stock, 1 cup at a time. After 20 minutes, add the pumpkin.

When the rice is cooked, stir in the cheese, butter, parsley and cream, if using. Ensure the risotto is soft, not solid. **SERVES 6**.

WINE MATCH

Pumpkin and Chardonnay are always good together. The sweetness of the pumpkin complements the ripe stone fruit flavours in this Lake Chalice Chardonnay while the richness of both makes for a sumptuous match.

Lake Chalice Chardonnay

An elegant wine with white peach flavours together with warm toasty oak from some barrel fermentation and ongoing maturation. Lots of creamy, buttery characters in both flavour and mouth-feel.

Marlborough-based **Phoenix Garlic Limited** was formed in 2006 by the Murphy and de Castro families who have been involved in the growing, packing and marketing of New Zealand garlic for more than 30 years. They are single-mindedly taking production into the future with new innovations and ideas.

Phoenix supplies local and international markets with world-class NZ Garlic and NZ Shallots. "Our goal is to provide a healthy quality product in a sustainable and efficient manner." Growers are accredited under New Zealand's GAP standard.

Lake Chalice

Established in 1989 by friends Chris Gambitsis and Phil Binnie, Lake Chalice is a local, privately-owned enterprise. Their range of wines has gained a high profile not just for their style and quality but also as a reflection of frontman Chris's obvious enthusiasm and dedication.

Combining the talents of winemaker Matt Thomson with the company's own grapes as well as fruit from selected growers, Lake Chalice offers a highly respected range of wines. From Sauvignon Blanc and Chardonnay, including their reserve Platinum and Raptor labels, to fresh, zesty Riesling, Pinot Gris and Pinot Noir, the company focuses on making quality, varietal wines from Marlborough grapes.

Lake Chalice is proud of its sponsorship of the Wingspan Birds of Prey Trust. Lake Chalice funds are used in to help injured birds and fund a captive breeding programme to re-establish the endangered wild falcon or Karearea. The presence of a falcon, a fierce and skilled predator, is welcomed in the vineyard as it can significantly reduce grape damage by preying on small birds.

Phil, his wife Sue, Chris and Matt are all keen sportspeople with a range of outdoor pursuits including road-biking, kayaking and competing in triathlons.

CHEESE

Long known as a source of superior seafood, the Marlborough Sounds are also home to a unique cheesemaking enterprise.

The art of cheesemaking has been carried out by the women in the Harper family for more than two centuries. Each cheese is handcrafted using traditional methods and local products: milk from the Linkwater Valley; salt from Lake Grassmere; and the olive oil rubbed on the rind of selected cheeses, from close to Blenheim. No synthetic flavourings, colourings or preservatives are ever added and all products are suitable for vegetarians.

Their Havelock cheese has been dipped in a 10-year-old, oak-aged, local brandy and wrapped in sweet chestnut leaves from the tree by the dairy door keeping the curd moist and creamy.

Havelock Apple & Cinnamon Galettes

1 sheet flaky pastry
¼ cup sieved raspberry jam
1 Granny Smith apple
1 teaspoon ground cinnamon
pinch ground cloves
Sherrington Havelock Cheese

Using a 7.5cm diameter biscuit, cut out 8 rounds of pastry. Brush with the jam.

Peel, core and thinly slice the apple. Place the slices over the pastry circles, overlapping them slightly like scales on a fish. Brush with more jam.

Preheat the oven to 180C.

Place the galettes on a baking paper-lined baking tray. Bake for about 30 minutes, until the pastry is crisp and the apples slightly browned around the edges. Lightly dust with the combined ground cinnamon and ground cloves. Serve with slices of Sherrington Havelock cheese. **SERVES 4**.

WINE MATCH

A unique and delicious cheese with firm earthy flavours. The sweet, ripe berry fruit of this Villa Maria Pinot Noir is a wonderful match for the savoury characters of the cheese.

Villa Maria Single Vineyard Taylors Pass Pinot Noir

A concentrated, full-bodied Pinot Noir with plenty of dark fruit flavours and aromas. Layered and complex but with a velvety texture and silky smooth finish. A very rewarding wine.

Adapted from a recipe for Stilton, the most famous of English blues, Sherrington Blue has a long-standing family connection. The cheese has a grey-blue rind and smells sweetly of mushrooms and wet straw. It complements game, mushrooms, fresh cherries as well as pears.

The Harper men have been making honey in commercial quantities for a decade. The bees feed on the native manuka (or tea-tree) producing a honey with a rich golden colour and distinctive aftertaste.

Sherrington Blue, Pear & Honey

1 wedge Sherrington Blue Cheese

1-2 pears, thinly sliced

3-4 tablespoons Sherrington Honey

Cut a piece of the cheese and top with a slice of pear and some honey. Enjoy as an appetiser or at the end of a meal. **SERVES 4-6**.

WINE MATCH

A match made in heaven – Villa Maria Noble Riesling with a fine blue cheese. The salty tang of the cheese and sweetness of the wine are wonderfully contrasting and the texture of both is very rich and satisfying.

Villa Maria Reserve Noble Riesling

This deep golden wine is a real treat. The aromas are apricot, orange zest, honey and citrus blossom while the rich, almost oily palate is hugely concentrated with a tremendous sweetness, yet balanced with Riesling's naturally high acidity. Divine.

GEORGE GERIS, SENIOR WINEMAKER, VILLA MARIA ESTATE

"I feel the magic of Marlborough food and wine begins with the breadth of food available. It's all right here, starting with the freshest shellfish and salmon. In addition, local breads, olive oils and fresh Farmers' Market vegetables along with salt from the local salt works, provide perfect appetisers for our ripe, intensely flavoured wines. A particular specialty, served to local and international winery guests, are mussels gently steamed in our viticulturalist's secret Sauvignon Blanc sauce and topped with fresh herbs. My personal favourite is local lamb rump, cooked rare and paired with any of Villa Maria's Single Vineyard Pinot Noirs. Mmmm – superb!"

Oat Biscuits for Sherrington Smelly Cheese

1 cup rolled oats

1½ cups flour

½ teaspoon baking powder

½ cup sugar

100g butter, cubed

1 tablespoon Sherrington Honey

1 egg, lightly beaten

¼ cup milk

Sherrington Smelly Cheese

Preheat the oven to 170°C.

Place the rolled oats in a food processor and pulse, until roughly chopped. Add the flour, baking powder and sugar and mix.

With the machine running, add the butter a little at a time, until the mixture is crumbly. Add the honey, egg and milk and combine to form a stiff dough.

Roll the dough out thinly between 2 sheets of baking paper, sprinkling with extra flour as needed. Cut into 6cm rounds and place on a baking paper-lined baking tray. Bake for 12-15 minutes, until golden. Great served under a slice of Sherrington Smelly Cheese. **MAKES ABOUT 30**.

WINE MATCH

This rich smelling, full-flavoured cheese benefits from a hint of sweetness in the wine, making this rich and textural Villa Maria Pinot Gris the ideal partner.

Villa Maria Single Vineyard Seddon Pinot Gris

Spices such as nutmeg, cinnamon and a hint of cloves come to mind, along with fresh, juicy pears. A richly textured wine making it smooth and weighty and giving a long, succulent finish.

The **Sherrington Grange Cheese Company** produces limited quantities of cheese. Their philosophy is that using old-fashioned care and traditional cheesemaking methods takes time but creates a better product. "Sherrington cheeses look, smell and taste the way they were meant to – a real taste of history."

Sherrington cheeses are available at the Marlborough Farmers' Market or order online. Sherrington Manuka Honey is available from selected supermarkets, the Farmers' Market or online.

Villa Maria Estate

In addition to producing an outstanding range of wines, Villa Maria is well known for three things. Firstly, the company, founded in 1961 by its current owner and Managing Director, George Fistonich, remains 100 per cent New Zealand owned. Secondly, Villa Maria has been New Zealand's leading wine award winner, both nationally and internationally since the early 1980s and thirdly, the company was the first in New Zealand to adopt screwcaps for all of its wines.

After extensive research in the 1990s, Villa Maria made the decision to introduce Stelvin screwcap closures across all ranges and declare the winery a cork-free zone on all wines produced as of the 2004 vintage. George Fistonich believes the consistency of wines under screwcap is one of the contributing factors to the company's increasing success.

Villa Maria offers four distinctive ranges – Single Vineyard, Reserve, Cellar Selection and Private Bin. Each range encompasses wines from New Zealand's leading grape-growing regions and focuses on an authentic representation of the grape variety and region in which it was grown.

Villa Maria's impressive Marlborough winery was opened in 2000, its much acclaimed design working in parallel with the surrounding landscape.

MUSSELS

Long savoured by Maori and those Pakeha keen enough to prise them from rocks on the seashore, the green-lipped mussel – the seafood aficionado's favourite – are now farmed in the clear waters of the Marlborough Sounds. Increasingly popular, they are served in top restaurants around the world.

Succulent, tasty Greenshell™ mussels are high in protein, low in calories, and provide many valuable minerals and vitamins.

One kilogram of mussels in the shell is equal to about 50 medium mussels. To open, place in two to four tablespoons of water or oil over medium-high heat. Frozen mussels in the half-shell add pizzazz to paella, risotto and soup and make appealing appetisers – just top and grill.

Mussels are also popular in a variety of marinades and perfect for salads, soups and savouries.

Mussel Fritters

300g Kono Tomato & Chilli Marinated Mussels

1 large shallot, chopped

2 tablespoons each: chopped parsley, coriander

salt and pepper to taste

2 eggs, separated

1 green pepper (capsicum), seeded and finely diced

½ cup each: self-raising flour, milk

oil for frying

Drain the mussels and pat dry. Place in a food processor. Add the shallot, herbs, seasonings and egg yolks. Blend, until fairly smooth.

Transfer to a bowl. Stir in the green pepper, flour and milk. Mix well.

Beat the egg whites until stiff peaks form. Lightly fold into the mussel mixture.

Heat a little oil in a non-stick frying pan. Place heaped tablespoons of the mixture in the pan. Cook until bubbles appear on the top then flip over.

Excellent served with a light salad and lime wedges as a light meal or a starter. **MAKES 12 FRITTERS.**

WINE MATCH

These fritters are delicious with a glass of wine in the early evening. The Tohu Sauvignon Blanc complements the slightly marinated flavour of the mussels and is perfect with the capsicum. A fresh and zesty pairing.

Tohu Sauvignon Blanc

The nose is dominated by lemon zest and green capsicum together with a hint of freshly chopped herbs. The palate is full-flavoured with a balanced acidity and provides a clean, fresh finish.

Marlborough Mussel Chowder

1 each: small leek, large celery stalk (including leaves)

2 tablespoon butter-infused rice bran oil

2 cloves garlic, crushed

¼ cup flour

1½ cups chopped Kono Mussels

½ cup white wine

salt and pepper to taste

¼ cup chopped parsley

1 teaspoon each: paprika, lemon juice

3 cups milk

Finely chop the leek and the celery (including the leaves). Sauté in the oil with the garlic, until the leek is soft.

Add the flour and cook for 1 minute, stirring. Add the mussels and white wine. Stir over low heat for 2-3 minutes.

Add the salt, pepper, parsley, paprika and lemon juice. Pour in the milk and heat until simmering, stirring frequently.

Great served with crusty bread. **SERVES 4.**

WINE MATCH

The creamy richness of the chowder is a wonderful match with this lighter style of Chardonnay. Both are very smooth with the Tohu Chardonnay being fruit-focused yet having enough fresh acidity to perfectly balance the dish.

Tohu Unoaked Chardonnay

This is a light to medium-bodied Chardonnay with lovely seamless fruit flavours and a good balance of acidity. With no oak involved, it ís pure fruit expression with a hint of creaminess and fresh, tropical tones.

BRUCE TAYLOR, CHIEF WINEMAKER, TOHU

"For me Marlborough means freshness, both in its great world-renowned wines and in its amazing fresh produce. Marlborough's famous Sauvignon Blancs like our Tohu have the fresh, clean fruit flavours perfectly suited to complement kai moana such as the green-lipped mussels of the Marlborough Sounds. A key part of my enjoyment of Marlborough food and wine is the strong association between our products, our pure clean waters and the crisp air. To see Marlborough on a spring day with snow on the ranges and budburst on the vines is to appreciate the purity and cleanliness of the environment that contributes so much to our local food, wine and quality of life."

Garlic Mussels

12 Kono Mussels in the half-shell

1 slice toast-thickness white bread

2 cloves garlic, finely chopped

2 tablespoons finely chopped flat-leaf parsley

3 tablespoons olive oil

salt and pepper to taste

Place the mussels on a baking tray. Separate the mussels from the shells, if preferred.

Discard the crust from the bread. Make coarse crumbs of the bread in a food processor. Combine with the garlic, parsley, olive oil and seasonings.

Sprinkle the topping evenly over the mussels. Cook under a medium-high grill until the crumbs are golden. **SERVE AS AN APPETISER.**

Alternative Toppings

Mussels with Hazelnuts: Combine 4 tablespoons of cold-pressed hazelnut spread (not the chocolate type) with 1 tablespoon of hazelnut oil. Dollop over 12 mussels in the half-shell. Grill.

Mussels Kilpatrick: Sprinkle 12 mussels in the half-shell with a little Worcestershire sauce. Dice 2 rashers of rindless bacon and sprinkle on top. Grill.

WINE MATCH

These easy nibbles are delightful with this fresh and clean-tasting Tohu Riesling, which is complementary to all three flavours.

Tohu Riesling

Both floral and citrus notes dominate this wine on the nose and on the palate. It is a very attractive style with an off-dry appeal balanced by a fine and fresh acidity. Ideal served chilled on its own or with a variety of dishes.

Kono New Zealand – owned by Maori, the indigenous people of Aotearoa – offers a premium range of Greenshell™ mussels including a choice of tempting natural and flavoured frozen products plus chilled, marinated delights. All are distinguished by a unique circular seafood logo and a harakeke band, representing New Zealand flax.

Kono, meaning 'food basket', is a traditional Maori woven flax basket used to carry, protect, and present produce.

Premium Kono Greenshell™ mussels – a seafood connoisseur's delight – are raised in the pure, pristine waters of the Marlborough Sounds, employing eco-friendly, sustainable farming practises.

Tohu Wines

Tohu (pronounced tor-who) is New Zealand's first indigenous wine company. It was established in 1998 and is jointly owned by the Wi Pere Trust (Gisborne), Wakatu Incorporation (Nelson) and Ngati Rarua Atiawa Iwi Trust (Nelson/Motueka). The company owns vineyards in Marlborough, Nelson and Gisborne focusing on producing single-varietal wines such as Sauvignon Blanc, Chardonnay, Pinot Gris, Riesling and Pinot Noir from Marlborough and Chardonnay and Merlot from Gisborne. Quality is paramount, and the emphasis on Maori and Maori culture gives the wines a unique and valuable point of difference.

Originally developed as a vehicle to take Maori values to the world, Tohu Wines have achieved considerable success. Production in the 2001 vintage was just 6,000 cases while in 2005 this grew to 60,000 and then for the 2008 vintage, more than 120,000 cases. Tohu wines are exported to more than 20 markets.

Tohu's symbolic label is taken from a section of a painting by prominent Maori artist Sandy Adsett and represents Aotearoa's tangata whenua (people of the land) by combining the land, sea and sky.

Marvellous Mussels

Rich in Maori legend, the alluring Marlborough Sounds are also rich in resources. Over 80 per cent of New Zealand's aquaculture exports are grown in the Marlborough region with Greenshell™ mussels, Pacific King Salmon, Pacific oysters, paua, and koura (fresh water crayfish) amongst the gourmet delights on the menu. And demand is increasing with export earnings from Marlborough produce exceeding $200,000,000 per annum.

For those who first set out in the 1960s to establish a mussel farming industry in the Marlborough Sounds it was far from plain sailing. While the deep, clean waters provided an ideal environment for raising mussels from spat (tiny baby mussels) through to harvest (twelve to eighteen months for 90-120 millimetre mussels) these modern-day pioneers had to navigate through numerous shoals – financial uncertainty, market uncertainties, modifying and inventing equipment and overcoming physical hardships.

But perseverance paid off. With the harvesting of the first big commercial crops in the Marlborough Sounds in 1977 mussel farming was beginning to prove it was a growth industry. One pioneer said that he hoped that farmed mussels would become as much a part of the New Zealand way as rugby, racing and beer. But in his opinion not all mussels were equal. The green-lipped mussel was a real delicacy and should never be confused with the bigger, rubbery blue variety, which he claimed could put people off all mussels.

The green-lipped mussel (Perna canaliculus) did indeed provide the kiss of life for the industry. Today, Greenshell™ mussels comprise the largest segment of the aquaculture industry with Marlborough contributing 80 per cent of New Zealand's exports to over 50 countries. Given the international popularity of the Greenshell™ mussel today, it is interesting to note that back in the 1980s this delight simply did not feature on New Zealand restaurant menus and shellfish lovers had to be content with oysters and scallops.

Versatile and easily prepared, Greenshell™ mussels, whether fresh or processed, are a home cook's delight. The plump, tender meat is creamy white if the mussel is male and apricot to orange if the mussel is female and the flavour of both is superb.

Marlborough mussel industry pioneer Keith Yealands was often quoted as saying, "It's not important where you start but it's important where you finish." New Zealand today has over 550 mussel farms totalling 4500 hectares, most of them in the pristine Marlborough Sounds. Large farms proposed for open coastal regions could result in a ten-fold expansion in the area in the near future. Clearly the mussel loving, green-lipped fat lady has yet to sing. The Greenshell™ show is far from over.

WALNUTS

When it comes to going nutty, Marlborough provides the perfect terroir. Walnut trees have been flourishing in and around Blenheim for generations. The mixture of wild-grown and Majestic Giant seedlings provides an interesting range of flavours.

There is an expanding market for top quality walnuts and the local industry is thriving. Perfect half nuts are packaged in clear plastic tubs, others are sold as pieces or cold-pressed into gold medal walnut oil or alternatively creamed into a spread.

Walnut spread is the perfect partner to blue cheese and figs or as a topping for seafood grills or ice cream. Walnut oil enhances stir-fried and steamed vegetables and adds nuttiness to dressings and bakes.

Walnut Tart

500g short pastry
160g Uncle Joe's Walnuts
1 vanilla bean
1¾ cups cream
1½ cups brown sugar
100g butter
2 eggs, beaten

Topping
¾ cup cream, whipped
1 tablespoon peach schnapps

Roll out the pastry to fit a 25cm flan pan. Chill.

Preheat the oven to 170°C. Place an oven tray in the middle of the oven to heat.

Lightly toast the walnuts in the oven for about 12 minutes, until golden. Cool, then coarsely chop. Place on the uncooked pastry base, piling more in the centre than around the edges.

Slice the vanilla bean in half lengthwise and place with all the remaining ingredients – except the eggs – in a saucepan. Heat to dissolve the sugar to make a butterscotch sauce. Cool then add the eggs. Remove the vanilla bean.

Pour over the walnuts. Place on the oven tray and fan bake for 1¼ hours or until just set. Cool.

Serve at room temperature in wedges topped with the whipped cream flavoured with the peach schnapps. **SERVES ABOUT 10**.

WINE MATCH

This stunning walnut tart is a real treat and a lovely way to end dinner. The beautiful perfumed flavours of the Huia Gewurtz add a new dimension to the dish and are further enhanced by the drop of peach schnapps in the cream.

Huia Gewurztraminer

On the nose this wine seduces with its rose petals and lifted aromas of warm spices, ripe pear and tropical fruit. The palate is rich with vanilla bean, orange and spices offering lots of complexity and great length.

Walnut Encrusted Fish

1 cup Uncle Joe's Walnuts, lightly toasted

1 tablespoon freshly ground black pepper

1 teaspoon ground cumin seed, toasted

1 teaspoon flaky salt

600-700g skinned and boned monkfish

3 tablespoons lemon-infused rice bran oil

Preheat the oven to 200°C.

Place the walnuts, pepper, cumin and salt in a food processor and pulse, until medium-fine.

Cut the fish into serving-sized pieces. Press the walnut mixture on to all sides of the fish.

Pan-fry the fish in the oil, until coloured and crusty. Transfer to the oven for about 5 minutes, until the fish is firm but not overcooked. Can be drizzled with a little extra lemon-infused rice bran oil or olive oil, if preferred. **SERVES 4**.

WINE MATCH

This full-bodied Huia Pinot Gris is a delightful combination with the fish and the walnuts, gently complementing the flavours rather than dominating them. Pinot Gris, with its milder fruit flavours, is often a great choice with milder tasting dishes such as this one.

Huia Pinot Gris

The aromas of this wine offer intense ripe pears, white peach and rich exotic spices. It has a lovely soft texture with layers of white fruit, nuts and spices and has excellent palate length and structure.

CLAIRE ALLAN, PROPRIETOR AND WINEMAKER, HUIA VINEYARDS

"I love cruising the Pelorus Sound with the family, stopping to harvest fresh green-lipped mussels and cooking them in a mixture of salt water and Huia Sauvignon Blanc with some chopped parsley and chilli. Then we eat the just opened mussels in their soup with crusty bread. Food and wine matching dinners at Huia with local chef Chris Gibbs are wonderful. He matches beautifully prepared fresh local produce with Marlborough's savoury Pinot Noirs and the beautiful zesty white wines. And growing a veggie garden is as rewarding as the vast array of Marlborough wines."

Pâté with Walnuts

16 Uncle Joe's Walnut Halves

¼ cup Uncle Joe's Walnut Pieces

3 tablespoons Uncle Joe's Walnut Oil

1 small onion, diced

350g chicken livers, patted dry

2 teaspoons ground cumin

1 teaspoon ground cardamom

salt and pepper to taste

¼ cup Kirsch

Lightly toast the walnuts under a grill or in the microwave for 2-3 minutes. Cool. Coarsely chop the ¼ cup of walnut pieces.

Heat the oil in a heavy pan and sauté the onion, until soft. Cut the chicken livers in half. Add to the pan and sauté for 2-3 minutes. Add the seasonings and kirsch. Heat through briefly then flame.

Place the livers and any pan liquid in a blender and mix, until smooth. Fold in the chopped nuts. Spoon into a ramekin and cool. Top with some of the walnut halves. Serve the remainder as an accompaniment. This pâté is excellent dolloped on the walnuts or crostini. **SERVES 6**.

WINE MATCH

Pinot Noir and pâté are often a good pairing as pâté can be quite rich and the acidity in Pinot can balance it. The cherry berry fruit characters of Pinot are also delicious with this starter.

Huia Pinot Noir

This wine shows intense aromas of black cherries combined with some floral character and smoky, almost savoury spice. The rich flavours include black berry fruits and warm toasty notes from the French oak. Beautifully balanced, smooth and delicious.

Uncle Joe's partners, Malcolm and Jenny Horwell, operate from a farm just north of Blenheim. They gather walnuts and hazelnuts in autumn and sun-dry them for six weeks before they are cracked.

The nuts are an excellent source of protective fatty acids and vitamins and Uncle Joe's additive-free walnuts, hazelnuts, spreads and oils carry the heart tick from the New Zealand Heart Foundation. Uncle Joe's Walnut Oil won the Best Walnut Oil and Best Oil in the Show at the Canterbury Royal Show in November 2007.

Huia

The warm, golden background and hallmark purple and white feather of the Huia label makes it instantly recognisable on today's crowded wine shelves. Claire and Mike Allan established Huia Vineyards in 1996 after working in a number of key Marlborough wineries and gaining extensive experience in Champagne, France.

Focusing mainly on aromatic styles, the Huia range covers six distinctive varietal wines: Sauvignon Blanc, Pinot Gris, Gewurztraminer, Riesling, Chardonnay, Pinot Noir and the elegant Vintage Huia Brut – a blend of Pinot Noir and Chardonnay made using the same traditional methods as those for Champagne.

The Huia was a unique New Zealand bird from the wattlebird family with pairs co-existing as a team in the dense forest canopy. It was incredibly rare and highly prized by Maori with its feathers used in ceremonial costumes. The last official sighting of the Huia was in 1907. However, there are unconfirmed reports of their birdsong being heard in the isolated bush of the Ureweras 40 years ago.

This small, family producer takes a very hands-on approach to their craft with the resulting wines reflecting all the care and attention lavished in both the vineyards and the winery.

GOURMET FLAVOURS

The idea of starting a Marlborough-based distillery for fruit brandies was first proposed in 1989 by a visitor from Alsace, France.

In Alsace, small mobile stills had been a traditional part of village life for many generations. However, the French government banned them after World War II and those that were not destroyed were moved into hiding.

'Alouette', as she was to become known, due to her French allure, was one such politically unacceptable still. She was smuggled across the Swiss border and legally shipped to New Zealand – and Prenzel. And the rest, as they say, is history.

Since then a wide, colourful selection of rainbow-hued fruit brandies, liqueurs and schnapps has kept connoisseurs happy.

Bruschetta with Citron Ice Feta Cheese

200g feta cheese
⅓ cup Prenzel Citron Ice
10-12 slices French bread
⅓ cup Prenzel Rosemary-infused Rice Bran Oil
1 cup cherry tomatoes, halved
1 cup watercress

Slice the feta cheese into 10-12 pieces. Place in a shallow bowl. Pour the citron ice over the top and marinate for at least an hour.

Place the bread on an oven tray. Brush both sides with the oil. Cook under a medium grill, until golden on both sides. Cool.

Drain the cheese and briefly pan-fry, until it just begins to soften.

Serve the toasted bread topped with the tomatoes, watercress and cheese. Can be drizzled with a little of the citron ice. **SERVES 4-5**.

WINE MATCH

Tangy feta cheese is great with Grove Mill Sauvignon Blanc, both having good levels of acidity and the tomato and watercress provide a delicious freshness and vibrancy.

Grove Mill Sauvignon Blanc

This is a fairly tropical style of Sauvignon Blanc but also has underlying herbaceous notes. Quite full and weighty with a pleasant citrus acidity and hints of grapefruit towards the finish. Lovely served chilled on a warm summer's day.

Butterscotch Tiramisu

2 large egg yolks
½ cup Prenzel Butterscotch
    Cream
250g cream cheese
1 cup cream
400g sponge cake
1¼ cups strong coffee

Beat the egg yolks and butterscotch cream over hot water, until light and smooth. Cool.

Slowly beat the cream cheese. Beat into the egg yolk mixture. Whip the cream until stiff. Fold into the egg yolk and cream cheese mixture.

Cut the sponge into shapes to fit your serving dishes. Place a layer in the base of each dish. Drizzle with coffee. (Sliced strawberries could be added if preferred.)

Spoon the cream cheese mixture over. Cover with more sponge and coffee. Top with more cream cheese mixture. Refrigerate for several hours before serving.

The top can be sprinkled with cocoa or coffee powder.
SERVES 8-10.

WINE MATCH

The creamy, buttery richness of this dish make it a good match with the weighty, smooth texture of this Pinot Gris and the butterscotch flavours complement the wine's elegant, candy-like sweetness.

Grove Mill Pinot Gris

A rich, sweeter version of this popular grape variety making it ideal with some desserts but also with terrines and pâtés. Concentrated dried pear and apricot characters that linger indefinitely and enough acidity to provide the ideal balance.

DAVID PEARCE, CHIEF WINEMAKER, GROVE MILL

"It is still possible take a bottle of white wine down to the beach and find a meal to go with it – fish, paua, mussels, pipis, limpets and the strange shell-less paua that is quite the aphrodisiac. You don't have to worry about pollution and the sun will probably be shining. The white wine to go with these will be good. I'm blessed with friends who give me wild pork, venison, tahr, rabbits, hares, goats, geese and ducks. The red wine to go with these will be good."

Mulled Wine Christmas Cake

1kg dried fruit mix

150g each: glacé red cherries, mixed glacé peel

100g each: pitted prunes, dried apricots, halved

½ cup Prenzel Mulled Wine Mix

250g (room-temperature) butter

1 cup firmly-packed dark cane sugar

2 tablespoons marmalade

1 teaspoon each: Prenzel Grand Orange Concentrate, vanilla essence

4 large eggs

2½ cups high-grade flour

Combine the dried fruits and mulled wine in a large bowl. Cover and marinate for 8 hours at room temperature. Stir occasionally.

Preheat the oven to 150°C. Lightly grease and line a 23cm deep, round cake pan with 2 layers of baking paper.

Using an electric beater, cream the butter and sugar in a large bowl, until light and creamy. Add the marmalade and essences. Beat well. Add the eggs one at a time, beating well after each addition.

Fold in the fruit and marinade alternately with the flour. Spoon into the prepared cake pan. Smooth the top of the cake. Bake for 2½-3 hours, until a skewer inserted in the centre comes out clean. Cover with foil and cool in the pan on a wire rack.

WINE MATCH

While a sweet dish and a red wine are not normally a good match, the dried fruit, cherries and spice make this partnership work well. The warm hints of cloves, nutmeg and cinnamon are lovely with this wine.

Grove Mill Pinot Noir

An almost savoury style of Pinot with underlying cherries and spices such as nutmeg. Plenty of nutty, toasty oak and a good weight and balance. A wine that will develop beautifully in the bottle.

The **Prenzel Distilling Company**, based in Riverlands Estate, won gold with their first Pear William Brandy at the world's largest open fruit brandy distillation competition in 1994. They now provide quality schnapps, premium vodka and brandies, unique infused oils and vinaigrettes, vinegars and toppings – literally something for everyone.

Prenzel have two retail stores/tasting rooms in Blenheim, one at Riverlands Estate, the other at The Vines Village on Rapaura Road. Eight other outlets are strategically located throughout New Zealand.

Grove Mill

Grove Mill was established in 1988 by a group of local winegrowers and wine enthusiasts. Located where the Waihopai Valley runs from the mountains to meet the Wairau Valley, the winery is surrounded by an attractive natural environment, which has driven the company's philosophy – to produce premium quality wines with minimal environmental impact.

As the first carboNZero winery in the world, Grove Mill helped establish this programme, which is managed by Landcare Research NZ. The company had to calculate, reduce and then offset their carbon dioxide emissions in order to qualify. This has further enhanced Grove Mill's commitment to caring for the environment, which is also symbolised by the Southern Bell Frog as the company logo. As well as living in the wetland surrounding the winery, frogs are good indicators of environmental quality due to their semi-permeable skin.

Grove Mill's range of wines includes Sauvignon Blanc, Chardonnay, Riesling, Pinot Gris, Gewurztraminer and Pinot Noir with grapes sourced from company-owned and contract vineyards throughout the Wairau Valley. Chief Winemaker, David Pearce joined the company at the outset, and while his first vintage was just 530 cases of Riesling in 1988, 20 years later it has grown to over 40,000 for the Grove Mill label.

Grove Mill also hosts The Diversion Art Gallery at their cellar door.

FLAKY SEA SALT

Marlborough is home to New Zealand's only producer of pure flaky salt. From the isolated windswept beach at Clifford Bay unpolluted sea water is drawn into the man-made ponds of Lake Grassmere and partially evaporated by the sun and wind.

The remaining water is evaporated in a dehydrator to produce tiny hollow pyramid-shaped crystals of salt prized for their natural flavour and soft texture. Marlborough flaky sea salt is as natural as the ocean, sun and wind used in its harvesting and it is Certified Organic by Bio-Gro New Zealand.

The delicate crystals dissolve easily so less salt is required (by weight) in cooking. Iodised flaky sea salt is also available.

Mini Feijoa Pavlovas

Pavlovas

3 egg whites

1¼ cups caster sugar

¼ teaspoon Pacific Salt Marlborough Flaky Sea Salt

2 teaspoons cornflour

1 teaspoon each: white vinegar, vanilla essence

4 tablespoons boiling water

Topping

2 cups cream

2 tablespoons icing sugar

6 feijoas, peeled and sliced

½ cup sliced strawberries, mashed

Preheat the oven to 190°C.

Place the pavlova ingredients in a large mixing bowl. Beat until the mixture is smooth, shiny and stiff, about 12 minutes.

Meanwhile, line one or two baking trays with baking paper. Lightly mark eight, 8cm-diameter circles on the paper.

Pile the meringue mixture into the circles. Bake for 5 minutes. Turn the oven off and leave for 1½ hours. Remove and cool.

Whip the cream and icing sugar until soft peaks form. Mash three of the feijoas and combine with the strawberries. Fold into the whipped cream. Dollop on top of the pavs. Garnish with the remaining sliced feijoas. **SERVES 8.**

WINE MATCH

The light and creamy texture of the pav and the fresh fruit flavours in the cream are terrific with this Gewurz – the flavours complementing the naturally exotic fruit in the wine together with its hint of sweetness.

Allan Scott Gewurztraminer

The perfumed, aromatic bouquet leads to a richly flavoured, spicy and floral palate with a lovely texture and mouth-feel. The flavours linger with this off-dry wine, endorsing its concentration of exotic tastes.

Preserved Lemons: First wash and dry Meyer lemons. With the tip of a sharp knife cut a cross lengthwise, almost through each lemon but not quite. They should hold together at the stem end. Sprinkle plenty of Pacific Salt Marlborough Flaky Sea Salt on the flesh. Place 2 tablespoons of Marlborough Flaky Sea Salt in the base of a preserving jar. Layer and lemons and flaky salt in the jar, squashing them down to extract juice. Sprinkle with a little more salt. Top up with lemon juice. Cover tightly. Stand at room temperature for 2 days, turning upside down occasionally. Refrigerate for 2 weeks before using. Thinly slice the skins as required – discard the flesh.

Chicken with Preserved Lemons

2 tablespoons lemon-infused rice-bran oil

1 large onion, diced

4 small poussin or 700g chicken portions

1 teaspoon curry powder

2 cups apricot purée

2 tablespoons sliced preserved lemon skin

freshly ground black pepper to taste

2 tablespoons cream

Heat half the oil in a large, non-stick frying pan. Sauté the onion, until softened. Remove to one side. Brown the poussin or chicken portions in batches. Return the onions to the pan with the curry powder and stir well.

Add the apricot purée to the chicken with the preserved lemon. Stir well. Cover and cook over low heat or in a 180°C oven for 1 hour. Season. Stir in the cream just before serving.

Sliced, preserved lemon skin may be used as a garnish.

SERVES 4.

WINE MATCH

This delightful lemony dish is great with Marlborough Chardonnay as they often have a predominant lemon citrus character. Slightly exotic, this dish is a treat with this oak-influenced Allan Scott version.

Allan Scott Chardonnay

Fresh lemons, melted butter and a toasted spice element all add up to a well-flavoured yet balanced wine. Soft and approachable, this is a wine for enjoyment on its own or with any number of white meat dishes.

JOSH SCOTT, WINEMAKER, ALLAN SCOTT FAMILY WINEMAKERS

"Luckily for me, Sauvignon Blanc is my drink of preference. When I first discovered or found my appreciation for Sauvignon Blanc I was working in Sancerre and Pouilly Fumé. Everybody talked about the match of goat's cheese (Crottin de Chavignol) and Sauvignon Blanc, how it was "made in heaven." However, I think the French were missing out. My perfect match for Sauvignon Blanc is seafood and we are very lucky here in Marlborough because we have bountiful fresh – and I stress fresh – local supplies of seafood. Scallops, oysters, crayfish, mussels, snapper, blue cod – all at our doorstep and a perfect match for our flagship wine. A coincidence?

Eggplant & Shallot Tart

400g eggplant, peeled and diced

1 tablespoon Pacific Salt Marlborough Flaky Sea Salt

¼ cup extra virgin olive oil

10 large shallots, thinly sliced

1 egg

2 tablespoons sour cream

¼ cup walnuts, finely chopped

Pacific Salt Marlborough Flaky Sea Salt and pepper to taste

23cm uncooked, thin pizza base

50g gruyère-style cheese, grated

Place the eggplant on paper towels. Sprinkle with the salt to reduce any bitterness. Stand for 20 minutes. Rinse and pat dry.

Preheat the oven to 220°C. Place a baking tray in the oven to heat.

Heat half the oil in a large frying pan and add the shallots. Cover and cook for about 20 minutes, stirring occasionally, until soft and light brown. Meanwhile, heat the remaining oil in another pan and stir the eggplant over low heat, until soft and cooked. Combine with the shallots. Cool slightly.

Mix in the egg, sour cream, walnuts, salt and pepper. Spread the mixture over the pizza base right to the edge. Sprinkle the cheese over the top. Place on the hot oven tray and bake for 15-20 minutes or until golden. **SERVES 4**.

WINE MATCH

This lightish dish needs a light-bodied wine to ensure it isn't overpowered and this Allan Scott Riesling is ideal. It also handles the slight nuttiness and sweetness of the gruyère very well as its style is off-dry.

Allan Scott Riesling

This is a light, lifted, floral style of Riesling with honeysuckle and citrus characters together with a refreshing acidity. Fine to enjoy on its own as an aperitif or with lighter dishes – an appealing wine, which is ideal for any occasion.

It was the Marlborough sunshine coupled with strong, drying nor'westerly winds and large areas of suitable flat land, that persuaded the late George W. Skellerup to establish his solar Grassmere salt works in 1943. Today, **Pacific Salt Cerebos Skellerup** continue to harvest this bounty from the sea.

The salt crust is lifted from the bottom of the crystallization ponds, washed in brine before being stacked in 20-metre high piles. The snowy stacks of salt are something of a landmark, readily visible from the Blenheim-Christchurch highway.

Some of this product is iodised and processed at the packing plant adjacent to Lake Grassmere.

Allan Scott Family Winemakers

Allan Scott began his career in the Marlborough wine industry in 1973, managing vineyards for a leading producer. In 1975 he bought land and grew grapes for sale under contract before building his own winery in 1990. It wasn't long before the range of Allan Scott Wines became well established both in New Zealand and overseas.

The Allan Scott wine business is truly a family affair with wife Cathy running cellar door facilities and the winery's popular restaurant, younger daughter Sara as the company viticulturist, son Josh as winemaker (and brewer of his own Moa Beer). Older daughter Victoria is involved in the promotion of the Marlborough region.

The range of wines produced by Allan Scott Family Winemakers encompasses Sauvignon Blanc, Chardonnay, Riesling, Pinot Gris, Gewurztraminer, Late Harvest Riesling and Pinot Noir in the 'estate' range plus a premium level with four single vineyard offerings and three sparkling wines made using the classic Méthode Traditionelle.

The company's eatery – the Twelve Trees Restaurant – was named after the original walnut trees that lined the Jackson's Road entrance to the winery. The trees were planted by a previous owner of the property nearly 75 years ago and remain a distinctive landmark.

OYSTERS

Anglo-Irish 18th-century satirist Jonathan Swift was brilliant with words but no gourmet. All lovers of good food would disagree with his claim that "He was a bold man that first ate an oyster."

Marlborough oysters are harvested from a new fishery at Cloudy Bay during November and December. They are the same species as their better-known Bluff counterpart and boast superb flavour, texture and size.

As well as tasting great, oysters are also extremely healthy containing glycogen, essential minerals, fatty acids, vitamins, plus well-balanced proteins, all essential for good health.

Foodies should note that the plump, succulent Marlborough Cloudy Bay oysters are 100 per cent natural – there are no artificial additives used during processing.

NB. Cloudy Bay Oysters and Cloudy Bay Wines are independent, unconnected operations.

Oysters with Asian Dressing

12 Talley's Cloudy Bay Oysters

2 tablespoons each: fish sauce, lime juice

dash sesame oil, optional

3 tablespoons salmon caviar or red lumpfish roe

small sprigs dill or fennel to garnish

Place the oysters in suitable serving dishes. Combine the fish sauce, lime juice and sesame oil, if using. Spoon over the oysters. Garnish with the salmon caviar or lumpfish roe and the dill or fennel. **SERVES 4 AS AN APPETISER.**

Alternative Oyster Toppings
- Balsamic vinegar
- Chopped chilli and Sauvignon Blanc vinegar
- Diced grilled bacon and grated Parmesan cheese
- Lemon juice and freshly ground black pepper

WINE MATCH

With its rich, toasty and obvious depth of flavour Pelorus is the ideal match with the firm Asian flavours used in this dish.

Cloudy Bay Pelorus

Intense and richly flavoured yet retaining a great elegance, Pelorus is a very expressive Méthode Traditionelle. From the toasted yet fresh aromas to the weighty palate with its flavours of citrus fruit and fresh-baked bread this is a wine with presence.

Oyster Soup

Stock
3 cups good fish stock
1 bunch fresh herbs
juice ½ lemon
freshly ground black pepper
  to taste

75g butter
½ cup flour
1 cup each: milk, cream
24 Talley's Cloudy Bay
  Oysters

Place the fish stock, herbs, lemon juice and black pepper in a saucepan over low heat for 10 minutes to allow the flavours to infuse. Cool then strain.

Melt the butter in a heavy saucepan and stir in the flour. Cook on low heat for 1-2 minutes. Gradually stir in the milk and stock, cooking until thick. Add the cream and the oysters.

The soup can be garnished with a little olive oil that has been infused with fresh basil leaves and strained. Drizzle in a circle in the centre. **SERVES 6.**

WINE MATCH

Te Koko, named after the scoop Tahitian explorer Kupe used to dredge for oysters in Cloudy Bay, is the perfect match. Its rich texture and flavours add a further dimension to the dish, leaving a lasting impression.

Cloudy Bay Te Koko

A unique wine and a very different style of Sauvignon Blanc. Richly textured with a nutty oak influence and lots of exotic fruits such as mango and passion fruit alongside freshly grated ginger, herbs and lemon zest.

Kevin Judd, Chief Winemaker & Managing Director, Cloudy Bay Vineyards Ltd

"Marlborough is about purity and vibrancy of flavour – our maritime climate with its clear air and high sunshine hours provides us with the conditions to grow grapes of extraordinary concentration and ideal natural balance. This intensely varietal fruit becomes the essential ingredient with which we produce deliciously crisp and flavoursome wines. Our pristine South Pacific environment also gives us the cool, clear waters of the Marlborough Sounds where the ultimate partners for our wines abound – fresh blue cod, mussels, scallops, oysters to accompany your favourite Sauvignon Blanc. And what could be better than salmon out of the smoker with a glass of Cloudy Bay Chardonnay."

Grilled Oysters with Cream

24 Talley's Cloudy Bay Oysters

50g butter, melted

1 cup cream

½ cup finely grated Parmesan cheese

The oysters can be cooked in shells on a baking tray or in individual serving dishes.

Cover the oysters lightly with the melted butter. Spoon the cream on top then sprinkle with the cheese.

Place the dish under the grill for 3-5 minutes or until the topping is slightly brown. Serve immediately. **SERVES 4 AS A STARTER.**

WINE MATCH

This is a rich combination – creamy, textural Cloudy Bay Chardonnay with the grilled oysters. Hedonistic and delicious. Delightful self-indulgence.

Cloudy Bay Chardonnay

This Chardonnay has a wonderful balance of power and elegance as rich, toasty flavours combine with the creamy texture and ripe, succulent fruit. Highly impressive while young but a wine that will age gracefully. This is a wonderful expression of Marlborough Chardonnay.

The **Talley's** seafood division has proudly evolved from its humble beginnings in 1936 in Motueka. The family-owned company now has a wide ranging involvement in the inshore, deep water and aquaculture industries.

Oysters are harvested from a new fishery at Cloudy Bay during November and December exclusively by Talley's Group Limited. The fresh Cloudy Bay oysters are delivered daily to ensure their full succulent flavour is retained. All shellfish are tested to ensure they are free of biotoxins.

Cloudy Bay

Without doubt one of the most well-known, high profile names in the Marlborough wine industry, Cloudy Bay is credited with putting Marlborough Sauvignon Blanc on the global wine map. Established in 1985 and now part of Moet Hennessy Estates & Wines, Cloudy Bay continues to make outstanding wines under the watchful eye of Chief Winemaker and Director, Kevin Judd.

In addition to Sauvignon Blanc, the winery's portfolio also includes Chardonnay, Pinot Noir, Late Harvest Riesling, and the exceptional sparkling wine, Pelorus, all of which are highly sought after by lovers of Cloudy Bay the world over. But there is one other wine – an alternative style of Sauvignon Blanc.

Cloudy Bay Te Koko was created by the winemaking team as an individual expression of the Sauvignon Blanc grape – a complex, savoury and full-bodied wine that is both aromatic and richly textured. Only released after considerable maturation, it has aromas of lychee and honeysuckle together with thyme and a hint of smoky oak. Te Koko is a limited release, very special wine found in some of the world's top restaurants and almost always at the cellar door in Marlborough.

FRESH HERBS & SALAD GREENS

Do you wonder how you ever survived without fresh herbs? For generations parsley, sage, rosemary and thyme – the herbs songs have been written about – flavoured our soups, salads and stews. Now we have an ever-increasing range of exotic flavours to savour. Coriander, basils, oregano, dill, tarragon and chervil all add their own unique characteristics to dishes.

And Marlborough's major local herb supplier also excels in growing salad ingredients such as mizuna, kamutzu, red kale, green frilly lettuce, rocket, fennel and sorrel.

Mesclun, a mixture of small salad leaves and herbs including rocket, curly endive or frisée, baby spinach leaves, mizuna, tat soi, baby beetroot, parsley, chervil or basil, is a popular mix with home cooks and restaurateurs alike.

Thai herbs such as kaffir lime leaves and lemon grass are also much sought after as are a dainty watercress and angelica.

Rocket, Asparagus & Goat's Cheese

8 stalks asparagus

2 cups Thymebank Rocket Leaves

6 each: cherry tomatoes, black olives

100g goat's cheese (eg chèvre)

1 teaspoon each: ground cumin, smoked paprika

¼ cup flour

spray oil

3-4 tablespoons herb dressing (page 70)

Trim the asparagus then blanch, until crisp tender. Refresh in cold water. Drain and pat dry. Arrange on two serving plates. Add the rocket leaves, halved cherry tomatoes and pitted black olives.

Cut the cheese into 2cm cubes. Combine the spices with the flour. Dredge the cheese in the flour mixture.

Spray a non-stick frying pan with oil. Heat until very hot. Quickly sear the cheese on each side for about 5 seconds, until just starting to melt. Place on the rocket and drizzle with the dressing. **SERVES 2 AS A STARTER OR LIGHT MEAL.**

WINE MATCH

This Astrolabe wine's more mineral and earthy components make it ideal with the ingredients in this salad. Goat's cheese and Sauvignon share a naturally high acidity so work very well together.

Astrolabe Awatere Sauvignon Blanc

A lifted nose of citrus, fresh herbs and minerals combine with gentle passion fruit notes, gooseberry and lime zest to give a complex, yet vibrant and refreshing style of Sauvignon Blanc.

Smoked Chicken, Fennel & Mesclun Salad

300g smoked chicken, sliced

1 small bulb Thymebank Fennel, thinly sliced

2 tablespoons lemon juice

1 teaspoon each: caster sugar, Dijon-style mustard

salt and pepper to taste

¼ cup olive oil

4 cups Thymebank Mesclun

Combine the chicken and fennel. Whisk the lemon juice, caster sugar, mustard, salt and pepper, until smooth. Gradually whisk in the oil. Sprinkle half over the chicken and fennel.

Place a large handful of mesclun in the centre of each plate and top with the chicken and the fennel. Drizzle with the remaining dressing. **SERVES 4 AS A LIGHT MEAL.**

WINE MATCH

Fennel, with its fresh hint of aniseed and the smoked chicken are a good combination and more than matched by this example of top Astrolabe Sauvignon Blanc.

Astrolabe Marlborough Sauvignon Blanc

A full-flavoured Sauvignon with plenty of ripe, juicy tropical fruit and a fresh undercurrent of fragrant herbs. Richly aromatic and loaded with flavours that linger indefinitely.

SIMON WAGHORN, WINEMAKER, ASTROLABE

"The Marlborough climate of warm sunny days and cool nights not only intensifies the fruit flavours of our wines, but also enhances the crisp, positive flavours of Marlborough's local produce. Like wine, I believe food should be simple to allow the quality and flavour intensity of the ingredients to shine through. There's nothing more lingering on the palate, than our Kekerengu Sauvignon Blanc with chilled oysters in the half shell, or our Awatere Sauvignon Blanc with steamed mussels sprinkled with fresh coriander and chilli olive oil from our own olive grove. Matched with friends on a sunny Marlborough day – perfection!"

Salsa Verde

5 cloves garlic, crushed

½ cup capers, rinsed and chopped

12 anchovy fillets, chopped

2½ cups (about 50g) each: Thymebank Flat-leaf Parsley, Basil, Mint Leaves, chopped

½ – ¾ cup lime juice

5 tablespoons olive oil

To make the Salsa Verde, combine the garlic, capers, anchovies, herbs, lime juice and olive oil.

Serve this zesty green sauce with fish, grilled chicken, steamed or grilled vegetables or on pasta or potato salads. **MAKES ABOUT 1½ CUPS.**

WINE MATCH

This flavour-packed sauce with its capers is a bit of a challenge for many wines, but good Sauvignon Blanc is by far the best choice, particularly if the salsa is served over fish or vegetables.

Astrolabe Kekerengu Sauvignon Blanc

Currant leaf, lime zest and dried herbs translate into an elegant wine with a flinty, mineral character and lingering flavours of peppercorns and gooseberry. Almost tangy on the finish, this is a vibrant and rewarding wine.

Many of **Thymebank's** salad ingredients and herbs are grown hydroponically in steamy tunnel houses to ensure an almost year-round supply. Over 54 varieties of herbs and salad leaves are provided to supermarkets, vegetable suppliers and restaurants throughout the South Island and lower North Island.

Thymebank is constantly experimenting with new herb and salad varieties – such as Texan tarragon (Mexican marigold mint) and horopito (native pepper leaf) – at its premises in Hammerichs Road. And local cooks are spoilt for choice because Thymebank will grow to order – courgette flowers are a particular favourite with German chefs in the region.

Astrolabe

Started by a group of friends in 1996, it wasn't long before this extraordinary label became a 'must have' in all serious wine retailers and top quality eateries. Primarily developed to provide winemaker Simon Waghorn with his own label, Astrolabe fast became one of the most sought after and respected producers in the Marlborough region.

Simon's long and productive history as a winemaker provided the ideal qualifications required to head up this range of wines. His passion and enthusiasm have led to an array of wines that slot perfectly into three ranges. Voyage: accessible wines offering archetypal Marlborough styles through astute viticultural management, fruit selection and intuitive winemaking. Discovery: wines that provide focus and clarity on Marlborough's fast-emerging sub-regions. Certainly regional and sometimes vineyard-specific, these wines highlight the attributes of individual sites and districts and their ensuing characteristics in the finished wines. Experience: wines in this range demonstrate Simon's innovative treatment of specific parcels of fruit and his willingness to challenge the 'everyday' winemaking process. Simon loves to experiment while capturing the raw, ethereal and sometimes undiscovered qualities of individual grape varieties.

One of Astrolabe's many achievements is the respect and delight garnered for its range of Sauvignon Blancs. Not content with just one Marlborough Sauvignon, Simon has produced outstanding wines from both the Awatere Valley and further south at Kekerengu.

FARMED VENISON

Lovers of gourmet meats can rejoice – top-quality venison is now readily available from supermarkets and butchers.

Farmed venison is natural, tender, mild, very healthy, delicious, extremely versatile, and suited to almost every cooking style.

Marlborough boasts several large landholdings where premium deer are farmed in open pastures year-round.

New Zealand farmed venison is produced without the use of artificial growth enhancers. It's naturally healthy, being low in fat, calories and cholesterol and high in protein with a great taste that just has to be experienced.

Cervena is distinguished from all other venison by the trademarked assurance that the meat has been naturally produced, and processed in accredited processing plants, according to a system of high-quality standards.

Thai-style Venison Salad

6 Premium Silver Fern Cervena Venison Medallions

1 tablespoon garlic-infused rice bran oil

salt and pepper to taste

1 shallot, diced

assorted lettuce leaves

2 tablespoons each: chopped mint, chopped coriander

1 small red pepper (capsicum), sliced

Lime Dressing

grated rind 1 lime

¼ cup lime juice

2 cloves garlic, crushed

freshly ground black pepper to taste

1 tablespoon fish sauce

2 teaspoons sugar

Brush the meat with oil and sprinkle with salt and pepper. Cook under a preheated hot grill or pan-fry for about 3 minutes each side. Allow to cool, then chill.

Meanwhile, soak the shallot in icy water to crisp.

To serve, thinly slice the venison and place over a bed of lettuce. Sprinkle with the mint, coriander, shallots and pepper.

Combine the dressing ingredients and drizzle over the salad. **SERVES 6**.

WINE MATCH

This is a zesty tasting salad and is therefore great with this fresh, young Nautilus Sauvignon Blanc. The coriander, red capsicum and lime juice in the dish are perfect with Sauvignon as are the other flavours.

Nautilus Sauvignon Blanc

Blackcurrant leaf on the nose as well as fresh herbs and fruit. This is a bright and vibrant wine with plenty of juicy red capsicum and ripe tropical flavours such as passionfruit and pawpaw. Ideal while young and fresh and a great partner for salads.

Venison & Udon Noodle Stir-fry

400g Silver Fern Stir-fry Venison

200g udon noodles

1 tablespoon each: olive oil, finely grated root ginger

1 red pepper (capsicum), thinly sliced

1 clove garlic, crushed

freshly ground black pepper to taste

3 tablespoons sweet chilli sauce

2 medium tomatoes, quartered

Pat the venison dry. Cook the noodles according to the packet instructions.

Heat a heavy frying pan or wok on high. Add the oil, swirling around the sides. Stir-fry the venison in batches, until seared but still a little pink. Do not overcook. Remove to one side.

Add the ginger, pepper, garlic and black pepper, stirring constantly. Pour in the chilli sauce and continue stir-frying for about 2 minutes. Add the tomatoes, venison and drained noodles. Cook for 1 minute to heat through. Serve immediately. **SERVES 4**.

WINE MATCH

Flavour is one aspect of matching wine and food and texture is another. The texture of these udon noodles together with the other ingredients and flavours is perfect with the richer texture of Nautilus Pinot Gris.

Nautilus Pinot Gris

This dryer style is packed with pears and ripe stone fruit and offers a delicate underlying minerality. Smooth and textural with lovely fruit weight and a succulent, long finish with hints of nutmeg.

CLIVE JONES, CHIEF WINEMAKER, NAUTILUS ESTATE

"Marlborough food and wine are absolutely world-class – the flavours, the ingredients, the reputation can all be enjoyed in a relaxed environment. For example, freshly steamed mussels on a boat in the Sounds with a glass of Sauvignon Blanc. Or a delicious bottle of Nautilus Pinot Noir alongside wild game caught in the hills and cooked on the barbecue or in a traditional hangi. The ambience heightens the enjoyment of the good things in life and when the food, wine and surroundings come together it makes for an unforgettable Marlborough experience."

Venison with Star Anise

3 tablespoons flour

salt and pepper to taste

3-4 tablespoons olive oil

1kg diced Silver Fern
Cervena Venison

2 each: black peppercorns,
star anise, bay leaves

⅓ cup crème de cassis

1 tablespoon Cabernet
Sauvignon vinegar

400g can tomatoes in juice,
chopped

Preheat the oven to 160°C.

Combine the flour, salt and pepper. Toss the venison in the mixture, pressing it in well.

Heat the oil in a heavy casserole. Brown the venison gently, a little at a time. Add all the other ingredients.

Cover tightly and cook for about 1½ hours or until tender. **SERVES 6.**

WINE MATCH

This combination makes the most superb menu for cooler evenings. Pinot Noir and aniseed flavours are very complementary and this Nautilus is no exception – rich, fragrant aromas and flavours that marry perfectly.

Nautilus Pinot Noir

Medium to full-bodied, this wine has tempting aromas of raspberry, cherry and spice while the flavours echo black berry fruits. Soft tannins and a balanced acidity make for a seamless wine with a long finish of cherries and chocolate.

Silver Fern Venison® represents tender, premium quality cuts produced to exacting specifications. The farm-raised venison is packed at dedicated production plants throughout New Zealand and exported worldwide.

The leafy fern depicted in the Silver Fern symbol grows freely in the native forests and bushlands of New Zealand. It symbolises the natural unspoiled environment of rich pastureland, rolling hill country and open plains where New Zealand deer herds are raised.

Farmers and suppliers are partners in Silver Fern Farms Limited, which is enjoying an international reputation as a supplier of premium New Zealand meats.

Nautilus Estate

Positioned at the western end of Rapaura Road, Nautilus Estate is easily recognised by the striking sculpture of a Nautilus shell, commissioned to celebrate the opening of the white winemaking facility in 2006. The shell was created by Wanganui artist Dale Hudson, and used over a kilometre of stainless steel rod and copper tubing and over 1000 spot welds in its creation.

Nautilus Estate owns a number of vineyards as well as drawing from contract growers for its fruit. The company's properties include 32 hectares of vines on classic stony Rapaura soil in Renwick, 10 hectares of picturesque glacial river terraces in the Awatere Valley, a 20-hectare block just across the Wairau River at Kaituna and the Clay Hills Vineyard in the eastern Omaka Valley.

Nautilus invests significant time and effort in researching the best combinations of site and clone for Pinot Noir. With the objective of improving the wine's fruit characters and intensity of aroma, the company has over 24 hectares of Pinot Noir planted in vineyards throughout the Marlborough region, in a variety of clones, some of which originate from Burgundy in eastern France, the spiritual home of Pinot Noir.

The Nautilus range of Sauvignon Blanc, Chardonnay, Pinot Noir, Pinot Gris and Cuvée Marlborough Brut are some of the most sought after wines both in New Zealand and abroad.

CHERRIES

Said to date as far back as 300 BC, cherry trees have been lauded for their sweet luscious fruit as well as for their beauty.

Marlborough is proud of its clutch of cherry orchards providing dark, deliciously succulent fruit during December and January. The unique Marlborough terroir that produces world-class Sauvignon Blanc and Pinot Noir also creates the remarkably intense flavour and colour that characterizes local cherries.

Visitors to the region enjoy 'picking their own' and for the Marlburians, packs of cherries are popular festive gifts for friends living out of the province.

Not only are they enjoyed fresh or frozen, cherries form the base of a very popular local harvest beer.

Cherry, Pear & Ginger Salad

½ cup Gewurztraminer or medium white wine

¼ cup crystallised ginger

2 small pears, halved and cored

2 cups Sujon Pitted Cherries

Place the wine and ginger in a small saucepan and bring to the boil. Remove from the heat and cool.

Add the pears and cherries and marinate for at least 30 minutes before serving.

Great served with crème fraîche or whipped cream.

SERVES 4.

WINE MATCH

The naturally spicy flavours of Te Whare Ra Gewurztraminer are great with this fresh, clean tasting dish. The ginger is perfumed and powerful but tamed by the pear while the succulent cherries provide wonderful flavour and texture.

Te Whare Ra Gewurztraminer

One of Marlborough's most famous Gewurztraminers, this wine has plenty of exotic fruits on the nose and palate including lychees, rose petals and orange zest. The flavours are rich and concentrated with a lovely hint of sweetness.

Creamy Cherry Pie

300g sweet short pastry
1 cup each: mascarpone and thick custard or
2 cups crème pâtissière
1 teaspoon vanilla essence
2 cups Sujon Pitted Cherries
1 cup Riesling
1 tablespoon powdered gelatine

Preheat the oven to 190°C.

Roll out the pastry thinly and line a 35cm x 11cm oblong, loose-based flan pan. Press a sheet of lightly greased foil onto the sides and base of the pastry. Bake blind for 12 minutes, remove the foil and continue cooking for a further 5 minutes. Cool.

Combine the mascarpone and custard – or the crème pâtissière – and vanilla to make the filling.

Meanwhile, poach the cherries in the Riesling for about 5 minutes. Drain and return the juice to the saucepan. Simmer for 2 minutes. Add the gelatine, stirring until dissolved. Cool, until just beginning to set.

Spoon the filling into the tart. Arrange the cherries on top. Spoon a little of the thickened juice over the top to glaze the cherries. Chill, until required. **SERVES 6-8.**

WINE MATCH

An unusual match but one that really works. The dish is not too sweet and the cherries really bring out the cherry flavour in the Te Whare Ra Pinot making for a very smooth, appealing and moreish partnership.

Te Whare Ra Pinot Noir

This wine has lifted aromas of ripe strawberry, black cherry and hints of mocha as well as violets and spice and plenty of cherry and plum flavours on the palate. Some almost savoury characters combine with the warm toasty oak on the finish.

ANNA FLOWERDAY, PROPRIETOR/WINEMAKER, TE WHARE RA

"What I love most about Marlborough food and wine is taking my girls to the Farmers' Market every Sunday morning and watching them taste and learn about all the great seasonal, local foods – breads, cherries, free-range eggs, game, Dorper Lamb – the list goes on. We joke that we take them to 'food church'. We love trying new things with them and then deciding what to buy and then involving them in the cooking. From the adult perspective we love trying to match our wines with new foods from the region – braised rabbit with the Pinot Noir, mussels with the Savvy and whitebait patties with the dry Riesling – heavenly!"

Cherry Sauce with Thyme

2 shallots, diced

3 tablespoons each: rice bran oil, citron ice, water

2 small sprigs thyme

2 cups Sujon Pitted Cherries

1 teaspoon butter

4 portions salmon fillet or groper (hapuku), grilled

Sauté the shallots in the oil in a frying pan, until softened. Pour in the citron ice and swirl to deglaze the pan. Add the water, thyme and cherries and heat through.

Serve over the cooked fish. **SERVES 4.**

WINE MATCH

This cherry sauce can work with any fish, but it is especially good with salmon and with Te Whare Ra wine's rich mouth-feel and clean, stone fruit flavours they make a delicious pairing.

Te Whare Ra Toru

This dry wine is an unusual blend of Riesling, Pinot Gris and Gewurztraminer – a lovely combination that is highly aromatic, has lots of flavours and is also textural. Fresh, lifted citrus and white stone fruits accompanied by an underlying mineral aspect.

The **Sujon Berryfruit Company**, a family business owned by pioneering Nelson berry fruit farmers Sue and John Gibb, is unique in New Zealand. Their berry fruit freezing and processing plant is one of the most modern in the world and uses sophisticated technology to freeze fresh berries down to minus 25°C in less than 6 minutes (conventional bulk freezing can take up to 12 hours). The result is berries that retain their character and texture, making them perfect for both professional and home cooks.

Much of Marlborough's cherry crop is purchased by Sujon. The cherries are mainly available to chefs and caterers; but the company is well known to New Zealand home cooks for their frozen berry fruits including boysenberries, blackcurrants, blueberries, raspberries, strawberries, cranberries, gooseberries and red currants, plus rhubarb.

Te Whare Ra

Te Whare Ra or 'The House in the Sun' in Maori, is home to Jason and Anna Flowerday and their four girls. It is the oldest boutique winery in Marlborough and was purchased by the family in 2003. With some of the oldest vines in the district and a long-standing reputation for producing fine aromatic styles, Jason and Anna focus on making wines with concentration, complexity and texture, while retaining finesse. In fact, some of the wines, namely Gewurztraminer and Late Harvest Riesling have become so sought after, they have developed a cult following and become collectors' items.

Both Jason and Anna are qualified winemakers. Jason learned his craft in Australia and Marlborough and Anna in Australia. She is the fifth generation of her family to be involved in the wine industry.

Te Whare Ra makes truly expressive wines with the well-drained, silt loams providing the ideal foundation. The family are careful to nurture this resource and are consciously working towards a more biologically sustainable system and reducing their use of chemicals wherever possible.

Though a small producer in the bigger Marlborough picture, the Flowerdays work tirelessly continuing to develop their dozen or so hectares to produce stylish, authentic wines that have a real presence.

SMOKED SALMON

Once a specialty food store item, smoked salmon is now readily available from supermarkets and delis. This delight can be savoured as cold smoked salmon, sliced or unsliced, hot (wood roasted) salmon, or enjoyed as gourmet bites, dips, strips and nibbles.

Smoked salmon is versatile. Excellent in soups, salads and mains, it also makes quick and easy finger foods for everyday entertaining: make smoked salmon 'roses' for topping crostini; roll around cucumber batons; or chop and garnish mini pizzas.

Dress up potato salads or omelettes with chopped smoked salmon; use in baked stuffed potatoes and serve with grills; or serve on toasted muffins under poached eggs and Hollandaise sauce.

And check out salmon caviar – a must for serving on oysters, crayfish, blini and vichyssoise.

Salmon Tartlets with Wasabi Mayo

15 small savoury tartlet cases

½ cup good mayonnaise

2-3 teaspoons wasabi paste

200g Regal Wood Roasted Salmon, cut into small pieces

Place the tartlet cases on a serving plate.

Combine the mayo and wasabi and place a dash in each case.

Top with the salmon and a dash more of the mayo combination.

May be garnished with herbs or watercress. **MAKES 15 SMALL SAVOURIES.**

WINE MATCH

The smoked salmon is great with the toasty complexity of the Family Estate Cuvée 10, which also balances the wasabi mayonnaise. A full-flavoured, satisfying match.

No 1 Family Estate Reserve Cuvée 10

A wonderful wine that offers great depth of body and flavour yet is seamless and rounded with great elegance. Dry with a fine balance of toasty, freshly baked pastries and fresh, clean and vibrant fruit.

Smoked Salmon Spring Rolls

200g Regal Cold Smoked Salmon

12 round rice paper wrappers

¼ telegraph cucumber, cut into sticks

½ red pepper (capsicum), seeded and julienned

2 cups thinly sliced iceberg lettuce

½ cup each: mint leaves, coriander leaves

Dipping sauce

¼ cup each: lime or lemon juice, sweet chilli sauce

Cut the salmon into 1cm wide strips.

Place 1 sheet of rice paper in a dish of warm water, until just softened. Place on a board.

Place a slice or two of the salmon, the cucumber, red pepper and a little lettuce on one edge of the wrapper. Add a few mint and coriander leaves. Fold in the sides and roll up enclosing the filling. Place on a platter and cover with a damp paper towel.

Repeat until all the rolls are prepared. Combine the ingredients for the dipping sauce and serve with the rolls.

SERVES 6 AS AN APPETISER.

WINE MATCH

These incredible spring rolls are so fresh and clean tasting and so easy. Delicious as a starter with a glass of Cuvée Number 8.

No 1 Family Estate Cuvée Number 8

A classic blend of Pinot Noir and Chardonnay, Cuvée Number 8 offers a full-flavoured glass of wine with lifted fruits tones and a toasty, nutty character. The constant stream of fine bubbles and great length of flavour indicate the high quality of this wine.

DANIEL LE BRUN, PROPRIETOR/WINEMAKER, NO 1 FAMILY ESTATE

"My choices of Marlborough food and wine matches are: (1) Wild oysters – the ones you can gather yourself on the rocks in the Sounds, and an unoaked Marlborough Chardonnay; (2) a rack of fallow venison – harvested in the hills – with a soft Marlborough Pinot Noir. To me nothing is more enjoyable than produce you have gathered from the wild and you can taste fresh, almost on the spot. Add some good friends and a glass or two of bubbles – even better!"

Salmon Pâté

200g Regal Smoked Salmon Pieces
100g cream cheese
⅓ cup cream
1 tablespoon lemon juice
½ teaspoon sugar
salt and freshly ground pepper to taste
2 tablespoons finely chopped chives

Place all the ingredients – except the chives – into a blender. Pulse, until smooth. Add a little more cream if too thick. Fold in the chives.
  Place in small bowls. Top with more chopped chives, freshly ground black pepper, rinsed and drained capers or Regal Salmon Caviar. This is a great spread for crostini, crackers or blinis. **SERVES 6**.

WINE MATCH

Bubbles and salmon always seem to go well together and the creaminess of this pâté and that of the Cuvée No 1 are wonderful. The fresh acidity in the wine also prevents the dish from being too rich.

No 1 Family Estate Cuvée No 1

This wine, made from 100% Chardonnay, is rich and creamy but with a fine balance of acidity. Very smooth with the tiniest hint of sweetness, this is a very easy wine to enjoy.

Regal Marlborough Salmon is a brand of the New Zealand King Salmon Company, which owns and operates all stages of farming, production and marketing. This ensures that they have total control and traceability of their products.
  Smoked salmon is cured in a wet brine then cold smoked for 12 hours at 23°C. Wood roasted salmon is also cured, hot smoked at 40°C for about six hours then further cooked for 40 minutes at 90°C.
  Regal also offers a wide range of different salmon snacks to suit every occasion.

No 1 Family Estate

Twelve generations of Champagne and Méthode Traditionelle production in France and Marlborough have made the Le Brun name synonymous with the production of fine, sparkling wines. Using only specialised equipment imported from Champagne, winemaker Daniel Le Brun continues the family tradition of handcrafting Méthode Traditionelle.

Established in 1999 in the Wairau Valley, No 1 Family Estate focuses on four very different styles of Méthode Traditionelle: the rich and creamy Cuvée No 1, a non-vintage blanc de blanc made from 100% Chardonnay; Cuvée Number 8, a non-vintage blend of Chardonnay and Pinot Noir; and Reserve Cuvée 10 and Cuvée Virginie (named after the Le Brun daughter). The last two are limited edition wines and made only in the best years.

Daniel Le Brun, a pioneer of the style in New Zealand, planted his first grapes dedicated to sparkling wine production in Marlborough in 1980. Winner of numerous awards and trophies, and New Zealand's only boutique producer focusing solely on Méthode Traditionelle, he continues to strive for the utmost in quality, year in, year out.

No 1 Family Estate is, as the name indicates, a family business comprising Daniel Le Brun and his wife Adele together with their daughter, Virginie and son, Remy. This is a family that excels at producing some of the best sparkling wines in New Zealand.

GOURMET VINEGARS

Grapes are one of the many fruits from which vinegar can be made. High quality Marlborough Sauvignon Blanc grapes are used to create a palate-pleasing white wine gourmet vinegar with deeply layered flavours. It is created using the time-honoured Orleans method.

Basically the Orleans method of making vinegar – first proposed by Louis Pasteur – involves trying to create the ideal conditions for the vinegar bacteria to make vinegar, as they would in nature. You provide them with food (the wine), air and a dark, warm environment. The long processing time produces flavours that don't develop when faster methods are used.

Cabernet Sauvignon Gourmet Vinegar has lingered in oak barrels for years. It has a wonderful aroma and a lingering taste with ripe berry and caramel notes.

Lamb Rack with Berry Jam Glaze

4 whole lamb racks, 3-5 cutlets per serving

1 cup berry jam

3 tablespoons Prenzel Cabernet Sauvignon Gourmet Vinegar

8 small sprigs rosemary

Preheat the oven to 190°C. Score the racks as for a ham and place in a large roasting pan, fat-side up.

Heat the jam in a small pan. Add the vinegar. Heat, then sieve. Brush over the lamb. Roast for about 15 minutes. Remove and tent with foil. Stand for 5 minutes before carving.

Cut the racks into serving-sized portions. Drizzle with a little of the jam mixture and garnish with the rosemary.

SERVES 8.

WINE MATCH

This fruit-forward Wither Hills Pinot with its ripe berry characters is perfect with the hint of berry fruit in the dish. Tannins in red wine also work brilliantly with the texture of red meat. A winning combination.

Wither Hills Pinot Noir

A bright and vibrant Pinot Noir with bramble jam fruitiness and an almost smoky character from the toasty oak. Ripe plums and well-integrated tannins make for a smooth and enjoyable wine.

Fettuccine with Smoked Ham

250g dried fettuccine

2 shallots, diced

2 tablespoons Prenzel Garlic-infused Rice Bran Oil

¼ cup Prenzel Sauvignon Blanc Gourmet Vinegar

250g smoked ham, thinly sliced

8 cherry tomatoes, halved

fresh herbs and freshly ground black pepper to garnish

Cook the fettuccine according to the packet instructions.
Sauté the shallots in the oil in a medium saucepan, until softened.
Add the vinegar and simmer until almost evaporated.
Stir in the ham, tomatoes and cream. Heat through. Serve over the drained fettuccine, garnished with the herbs and pepper. **SERVES 2**.

WINE MATCH

The creamy nature of the dish is akin to the creamy, buttery characters of this full-bodied Wither Hills Chardonnay and the smoky ham works well with the oak influence in the wine. The rich textures are perfect together too.

Wither Hills Chardonnay

This full-bodied style with sweet, ripe fruit is a must for lovers of big Chardonnay. Plenty of toasty oak with cashew nut flavours and juicy golden peaches balanced by a fine acidity and a warm, lingering finish.

BEN GLOVER, CHIEF WINEMAKER, WITHER HILLS

"Marlborough is about purity, cleanliness, intense flavours, clear skies, valleys and ranges, crayfish, scallops, mussels, fishing with kids off the wharf, what you catch, real, fresh food prepared simply. It's about the spectacular view from the air as you fly into Marlborough, contrasting colours, ever-changing vistas. It's about new vineyards in all directions, the short history of Marlborough and wine, the Wither Hills standing guard over the lower Wairau Valley, the coast, whitebait, red sunsets, glossy Marlborough Sounds water, the hype during harvest, camaraderie, no two years the same and the challenge of striving to make the perfect wine."

Grilled Monkfish with Herb Dressing

Herb Dressing
½ cup Prenzel Sauvignon Blanc Gourmet Vinegar
2 shallots, finely diced
2 cloves garlic, crushed
1 teaspoon each: dried thyme, basil, marjoram
salt and pepper to taste
1 cup extra virgin olive oil
2 teaspoons Dijon mustard

750g skinned and boned monkfish

Whisk the vinegar, shallots, garlic, herbs, salt and pepper, until well combined. Cover and keep in a cool place for about 8 hours. Strain the mixture.

Whisk the oil and mustard into the strained vinegar. Cover and refrigerate, until ready to use.

Cut the fish into serving-sized pieces. Marinate in a ½ cup of the herb dressing for about 30 minutes. Drain then grill or barbecue for about 4-5 minutes each side, brushing with the dressing during cooking.

The dressing is also great on tossed salads, pasta salads or hot potatoes. **THE DRESSING MAKES ABOUT 1½ CUPS. FISH SERVES 4.**

WINE MATCH

Sauvignon Blanc and fish are always good together and the herbs in the dressing accentuate the wine's flavours even more. The nature of Wither Hills Sauvignon Blanc makes it ideal with delicate fish dishes.

Wither Hills Sauvignon Blanc

One of the most popular Marlborough Sauvignon Blancs, this is a full-flavoured, ripe and juicy style of wine. Tropical fruit such as guava and melon go hand in hand with citrus tones such as lime and grapefruit together with a lifted acidity.

The **Prenzel Distilling Company** has a range of vinegars that are quite unlike any other on the market.

"Prenzel vinegars taste as they did to the medieval palate, with a wide range of layered flavours and subtleties. No attempt is made to sugar or otherwise soften the product – it is just pure vinegar with no chemical additives of any kind."

Peta Mathias, Chef and TV Food Stylist and Presenter.

Wither Hills

Established in 1992, Wither Hills has enjoyed significant growth to become one of the region's most successful producers.

Just one kilometre from Blenheim's town boundary, the company's iconic winery and cellar door opened in March 2005. The considered and elaborate design blends with the backdrop of the majestic Wither Hills. Consisting of several storeys including an underground barrel hall that doubles as an atmospheric dining room – the building is a popular venue for functions.

The winemaking team, led by Chief Winemaker Ben Glover work hard to maintain quality and consistency while constantly evolving the Wither Hills' style. The ongoing development of the company's vineyard sites within the Wairau Valley provides the team with a range of individual characteristics and flavour profiles to work with.

Wither Hills focuses on a core range of Sauvignon Blanc, Chardonnay and Pinot Noir, each highlighting the team's attention to detail and quality, while echoing the key characteristics of Marlborough. These wines can now be found across the globe, featuring in North and South America, Asia, Europe and the UK.

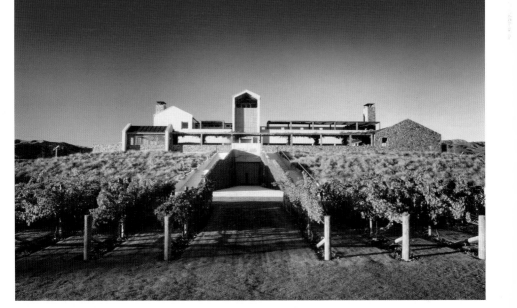

OLIVE OIL

The late Professor Gidon Blumenfeld, "the Grandfather of the New Zealand olive industry", planted the first commercial grove in Marlborough in 1986. He and his wife Triska were dedicated visionaries. The first tangible sign of their dream becoming a reality came in 1991 when they produced a small quantity of fine olive oil with a modest imported traditional press. This first oil pressed by the professor has become a collector's item. The company is now owned by a group of growers and the oil is pressed in central Blenheim.

The 'new world' environment in which the olives are grown creates a unique 'drizzling' oil, high in nutritious oleic acid. The combination of 'young' soil, extreme temperatures and a clean environment produces an oil with fresh herbaceous characters.

Chardonnay-dressed Crayfish

1 small fennel bulb
1 small fresh red chilli, seeded and chopped
2 spring onions, finely chopped
⅓ cup Blumenfeld Extra-Virgin Olive Oil
½ cup each: Chardonnay, cream
1 teaspoon cornflour
600-700g crayfish or 400 skinned and boned white fish

Discard the stalks from the fennel bulb. Halve the bulb lengthwise, core, and thinly slice crosswise.

Add the fennel, chilli and spring onions to the oil in a heavy frying pan. Stir over medium-high heat, until the fennel begins to soften, about 4-5 minutes. Add the Chardonnay and bring to the boil.

Combine the cream with the cornflour and stir into the sauce. Simmer until thickened. Serve over the cooked fish. (Cook the crayfish using your preferred method. Cook the fish by pan-frying in a little olive oil.) **SERVES 2**.

WINE MATCH

Rich, creamy Whitehaven Chardonnay is wonderful with crayfish and even better with this delicate but richly textured sauce. Both have subtle flavours and a delightful richness.

Whitehaven Chardonnay

Medium-bodied and packed with a balance of ripe fruit and toasty oak characters, this is a very rewarding Chardonnay. Deliciously smooth and with a hint of fine acidity, it is ideal either on its own or with food.

Aioli

2 plump cloves garlic, peeled

1 egg yolk

salt and white pepper to taste

2 tablespoons lemon juice

1 teaspoon each: Dijon-style mustard, caster sugar

¾ cup Blumenfeld Extra Virgin Olive Oil

Place the garlic in a blender and mix, until smooth. Whisk the egg yolk then add to the garlic with the salt, pepper, lemon juice and mustard. Mix until smooth.

With the motor running, slowly drizzle in the oil in a steady stream. Continue mixing, until thick.

Serve in a bowl with side dishes of fresh vegetables for dipping such as snow peas, celery sticks, blanched asparagus and beans, baby carrots, cherry tomatoes and red and green peppers (capsicums). The dip may be stored covered, in the refrigerator, for up to 3 days but is best enjoyed fresh. **MAKES ABOUT 1 CUP.**

WINE MATCH

This full-flavoured garlicky aioli and the crunch of the fresh vegetables for dipping need a refreshing, zesty wine, which is exactly what the Whitehaven Sauvignon Blanc is.

Whitehaven Sauvignon Blanc

Fresh, lifted and vibrant, this full-flavoured Sauvignon Blanc is great on its own or with food. Tropical fruit characters on the nose and echoed on the palate together with freshly chopped capsicum.

SUE WHITE, DIRECTOR, WHITEHAVEN WINE COMPANY LTD

"I really appreciate the variety of locally-produced food that's available. The four distinct seasons mean there is always something to look forward to. We're lucky to have growers supplying us who are also the hunting/shooting types and they're generous with their booty. Our Pinot Noir with its rich fruit flavours goes beautifully with venison or rabbit. Summer here means fresh, crisp, green salads and Sauvignon Blanc. Everything grows here, and local asparagus and new potatoes alongside the best Marlborough Sounds salmon is a perfect summer meal accompanied by our capsicum-flavoured Sauvignon Blanc."

Cervena Bites with Olive Oil & Saffron

500g minced (Cervena) venison

4 tablespoons chopped fresh Italian parsley

2 cloves garlic, chopped

1 small egg

salt and pepper to taste

flour for dusting

¼ cup Blumenfeld Extra Virgin Olive Oil

2 shallots, diced

½ cup each: beef stock, Pinot Noir

¼ teaspoon each: paprika, saffron threads

Combine the venison, 1 tablespoon of the parsley, half the garlic, the egg and seasonings in a food processor. Blend, until well mixed. Roll into 2.5cm balls. Dust with flour. Set aside.

Heat the oil in a heavy frying pan over medium-high heat. Add the meatballs and sauté until browned all over, about 8 minutes. Using a slotted spoon, transfer the meatballs to a plate.

Add the shallots to the pan. Sauté on medium heat, until tender. Stir in the stock, wine, paprika and saffron. Return the meatballs to the pan, cover and simmer, until tender, about 25 minutes. Uncover, add the remaining parsley and garlic. Simmer, until thickened. **SERVES 6 AS A STARTER.**

WINE MATCH

These succulent, well-flavoured little meatballs have a great texture that loves the tannin in the Whitehaven wine. The flavours are perfect together – meaty but with a bit of spice and lovely balancing acidity.

Whitehaven Pinot Noir

Dark fruits such as plums and black cherries come to mind with the aromas of this wine. Quite full-bodied with a lovely velvety texture and the ripe forest fruits and balanced structure make for a great wine.

Blumenfeld is now owned and supported by over 25 private olive estates from throughout New Zealand. The brand has become one of New Zealand's largest olive oil companies. The partners work co-operatively to share experience and strengths to produce a premium condiment oil for the international market.

Blumenfeld won the Best Extra Virgin Olive Oil International Award at the prestigious LA County Fare, and Best Olive Oil at the Olive Business 2003 Olive Oil Awards, Melbourne. The Supreme Champion Oil was created from olive cultivars introduced by the late Professor Gidon Blumenfeld and consists of a Frantoio, Leccino, Picholine and Koroneiki blend.

Whitehaven

Following careers in finance and marketing, Greg and Sue White decided to do what many dream of but few achieve – chuck it all in and go sailing. Their adventures took them through the Pacific and around New Zealand's coastline before mooring in the Marlborough Sounds for three months. After a foray ashore and a few local Sauvignon Blancs, the pair decided to remain on dry land and in 1994 the Whitehaven Wine Company was born.

Initially based in Blenheim, by 2001 it became clear that the old boutique winemaking facilities were no longer suitable for Whitehaven's growing production and the company purchased 16 hectares off Rapaura Road, Renwick and built a new winery capable of processing 5000 tonnes. From their first production of 5,000 cases in 1995 to 200,000 cases in 2008, Whitehaven has undergone some serious growth and is now distributed in New Zealand, Australia, the United Kingdom, Ireland, Hong Kong, Japan, the United States and Canada.

The range of wines produced by Whitehaven includes Pinot Noir, Pinot Gris, Gewurztraminer, Riesling, Chardonnay and the company's flagship Sauvignon Blanc.

Though having undergone significant growth, the Whitehaven team remains small and focused on the goal of producing elegant, fine wines with distinctive regional character.

HONEY & HAZELNUTS

Growing hazelnuts is a tough nut to crack: the trees need long hot summers and crisp, frosty winters to produce premium quality nuts; it takes six years before the trees are commercially viable; the nuts are often harvested by hand in late summer and early autumn, then graded; the hard outer shells – the shape is a cross between a helmet and an acorn – are cracked in winter and the nuts processed and packed.

Marlborough's busy bee population thrives on pollen from the fragrant flowering cherries and stone fruit trees, myriad crops with flowers plus the manuka on the hills. There are several long-standing apiaries that produce a variety of honeys to be enjoyed, available from the Farmers' Market or selected supermarkets.

Mussels In Hoisin & Honey Sauce

24 Kono Mussels
2 tablespoons canola oil
1 tablespoon grated root ginger
2 cloves garlic, crushed
2 tablespoons each: hoisin sauce, honey
1-2 tablespoons lime juice
chopped coriander to garnish
8 lemon wedges

Scrub the mussels and remove the beards.

Heat the oil in a large, heavy-based saucepan or wok. Stir in the ginger, and garlic. Add the mussels, stir briefly then cover and cook for 4-5 minutes, until opened. Remove the mussels as they open. Discard any mussels that do not open. If they open just a little then they are still edible. Return all the opened mussels to the pan and add the hoisin sauce, honey and lime juice and heat through.

Remove the black foot in the mussels, if preferred. Serve in individual bowls drizzled with a little of the cooking liquid and coriander. Serve accompanied by the lemon wedges.

SERVES 4 AS A STARTER.

WINE MATCH

While this Forrest Riesling is a dry wine, it has lots of flavour including a hint of honey. It loves Asian flavours such as this mussel dish and adds its own hint of lime zest.

Forrest The Valleys
Wairau Valley Dry Riesling

With aromas of nectarine, citrus zest and a flinty minerality, this finely-honed wine offers a great balance of ripe, juicy fruit with a fine, bright acidity. Dry yet beautifully textural and with a long finish reminiscent of lime cordial.

To roast hazelnuts, place in a pan in the oven at 180°C for about 10 minutes or until lightly coloured. Cool slightly then tip into a large sieve and shake them. This should remove most of the skins. Rub the rest off with a clean tea towel.

Berry Baskets

⅓ cup rice bran oil

8 sheets filo pastry

2 cups mascarpone

¼ cup toasted hazelnuts, chopped

1 tablespoon honey

2 cups each: blueberries, raspberries

Preheat the oven to 190°C. Place an oven tray in to heat. Lightly brush 8 ramekins or an 8-hole Texas muffin pan with oil.

Cut each sheet of filo in half crosswise then cut each half into quarters about 14cm x 14cm square. Lightly oil each square. Pile four squares one on top of the other. Line the ramekins with the filo.

Place on the hot baking tray and bake for 8 minutes, until golden. Cool.

Combine the mascarpone with the hazelnuts and honey. Fill the baskets. Serve topped with the berries. **SERVES 8**.

WINE MATCH

Forrest The Doctors' Riesling

The amount of sweetness in this Forrest Riesling is perfect with this not-so-sweet dessert. The fresh berry flavours and creamy mascarpone taste wonderful when enjoyed with the citrusy characters and delicate acidity of the wine.

Lime sorbet and juicy green apples on the nose then flavours of dried apricot, spices and mango. Some sweetness balanced by a fine acidity and the wine's naturally lower alcohol adds to its appeal.

JOHN FORREST, CHIEF WINEMAKER AND PROPRIETOR, FORREST ESTATE

"What excites me about Marlborough's wine and food is minerality. Tasting our marvellous cuisine and wine it's this mineral, almost salty character from the Wairau Valley stony 'terroir' mirrored in the food. My favourite is whitebait, caught at the mouth of the Wairau River, with my dry Riesling. That 'wet stone' aroma as you scoop your net into the river to snare a precious shoal is identical to that arising from a stony vineyard as you wander through sampling grapes – so evocative! When I finally cook my hard-earned catch it's just whitebait, eggs, dash of milk, pinch of salt and fried lightly golden in butter. With a glass of dry Riesling of course!

Hazelnut Bread & Butter Puddings

4 eggs

⅓ cup sugar

¾ cup milk

½ cup cream

3 tablespoons honey

5 toast-thickness slices white bread

25g butter, softened

¼ cup ground roasted hazelnuts

2-3 tablespoons icing sugar

Lightly grease six individual soufflé dishes or ramekins.
Whisk together the eggs, sugar, milk, cream and honey.
Set aside.

Remove the crusts from the bread then lightly spread with the butter. Cut into cubes. Line the bottom of the prepared soufflé dishes with bread. Sprinkle with the hazelnuts. Top with the remaining bread.

Pour the liquid mixture evenly over the bread and leave for at least 1 hour.

Preheat the oven to 150°C. Fan-bake the pudding for about 20 minutes. Remove from the oven and dust with icing sugar. **SERVES 6**.

WINE MATCH

When matching wine to desserts, the wine should be sweeter than the dish. Here the rich texture and concentrated flavours of this Forrest Riesling are delightful with the toasty, honeyed flavours in the bread and butter pudding.

Forrest Botrytis Riesling

Rich, lusciously sweet and jam-packed with apricots, orange marmalade, honey, mango, citrus blossom and more. Divine served slightly chilled with creamy, honey or stone fruit desserts or with blue cheese.

Marlborough's hazelnut growers roast and skin a selection of their nuts and sell them – plus the raw nuts – to delis and good food stores throughout the country. They are also sold internationally. Lower grade nuts are turned into gluten-free flour, paste, or dukkah or roasted and seasoned. There is also an excellent hazelnut oil, which, although expensive, is perfect in salad dressings or just sprinkled over steamed green vegetables.

Forrest Estate

A passion for wine enticed Drs John and Brigid Forrest to relinquish their respective careers in biology and medicine and return to Marlborough in 1988 to establish their vineyard in the heart of the stony Wairau River Valley.

John's mission is to reflect the geography of his native Marlborough in each of his wines. This focus on 'terroir' – the site, soils and micro-climate of each vineyard – contributes varying complexities to the resulting wines.

Nowhere is this truer than with Forrest Rieslings. With five in the range this grape variety is clearly the obsession of John and his team. Whether dry as in the Wairau Valley, off-dry such as the Forrest label, medium as in The Doctor's or richly sweet as in the Late Harvest and Botrytis styles, each is an authentic representation of Riesling at its best.

Sauvignon Blanc is of course key to any Marlborough producer and this is also true at Forrest. The desire to highlight 'terroir' contribution, particularly the stony Wairau riverbed, results in a Sauvignon with tremendous elegance and structure but with more subtle aromas and flavours such as thyme and sage with citrus fruits, elderflower and an underlying, gentle tropical note.

Forrest Sauvignon Blanc is also created to flourish with age so will reward drinking in its youth as well as after some years in the bottle.

Vines of plenty – Awatere Valley

127

The West Coast of the South Island is famous for its whitebait. But, one of Marlborough's best kept secrets is that the lower Wairau River is also great for whitebaiting.

Fritters are a favourite but here are some other serving suggestions:

- Dust in flour and quickly stir-fry in a little butter, add 3 cloves of chopped garlic, the juice of a lemon, some chopped parsley then serve.
- Combine with cream and eggs and seasonings and bake in a pastry case to make a whitebait quiche.
- Add to omelettes.
- **Whitebait Roulade**. Combine 250g of whitebait with 4 egg yolks, a ¼ cup of cream and salt and pepper to taste. Fold in the 4 stiffly beaten egg whites. Bake in a baking paper-lined Swiss roll pan at 200°C for 10 minutes. Cool. Turn onto a board. Thinly spread with cream cheese, sprinkle with finely grated Parmesan cheese and roll up. Served sliced accompanied by a crisp salad and tangy dressing.

Whitebait Fritters

250g whitebait

2 tablespoons flour

4 tablespoons milk

2 large eggs, separated

salt and pepper to taste

1 kaffir lime leaf, finely julienned or

2 teaspoons finely grated lime rind, optional

rice bran oil for frying

2 lemons, cut into wedges

Rinse the whitebait and pat dry with paper towels.

Whisk the flour and milk until smooth then beat in the egg yolks, salt and pepper. Add the kaffir lime leaf or lime rind, if using.

Whisk the egg whites, until stiff. Fold in the flour mixture and the whitebait.

Heat 1-2 tablespoons of the oil in a non-stick frying pan. Shallow-fry heaped tablespoons of the whitebait mixture, until golden on both sides.

Drain on paper towels. Serve immediately with lemon wedges. **SERVES 6 AS A STARTER.**

WINE MATCH

These fritters are ideal with a fresh, youthful white wine such as Sauvignon Blanc or Riesling. Both varietals have a zesty acidity to match the lemon juice that is squeezed over the top, while the flavour profile is lively and refreshing.

Marlborough figs are another treat and many backyards sport a tree or two. Local fig farms supply a few restaurants and fruit stores in the surrounding regions. Again, the Farmers' Market is a great place to taste and buy – or you can always ask your neighbour.

Zesty Grilled Figs

1 teaspoon finely grated orange rind

½ cup orange juice

½ teaspoon each: lemon juice, vanilla essence

2 tablespoons each: sugar, finely chopped mint

6 large but firm figs

4 ripe apricots

1 cup raspberries

6 tablespoons brown sugar

Combine the orange rind, citrus juices, vanilla essence, sugar and mint in a bowl.

Halve or quarter the figs. Halve and stone the apricots. Divide the fruit between four grill-proof dishes.

Just before serving, sprinkle the fruit with the citrus/sugar mixture. Caramelise with a blowtorch or place under a very hot grill until the fruit is slightly scorched. **SERVES 4.**

WINE MATCH

This lovely sweet yet fresh combination would be delicious served with a Late Harvest wine. Made from grapes that are ultra-ripe, these wines have a rich sweetness but also a refreshing acidity, which prevents them from being cloying.

Baked Figs with Goat's Cheese

6 large figs (not too soft)

50g goat's milk feta cheese, cut into 6 pieces

¼ cup each: Prenzel Crème de Cassis, Cabernet Sauvignon Vinegar

Preheat the oven to 190°C.

Make two cuts in the figs at right angles to each other, cutting from the top to halfway down. Insert a piece of goat's cheese in the cut. Drizzle with a little of the combined cassis and vinegar.

Bake for 10 minutes until the cheese has just begun to soften. Baste once during cooking.

Serve the figs in the centre of small plates and drizzle a little of the cooking juices over the top and around the outside. **SERVES 6 AS A STARTER.**

WINE MATCH

A medium-style Riesling or Pinot Gris would be the perfect match for this blend of sweet and savoury flavours. The wine needs some sweetness to match the figs, but not so much that you lose the delicate taste of the goat's cheese.

Harvest Grape Cake

This cake is great prepared with the 'thinnings' from the grape harvest or small table grapes.

1½ cups self-raising flour

1 teaspoon salt

¼ teaspoon baking soda

50g butter, softened

¾ cup sugar

3 tablespoons extra virgin olive oil

2 large eggs

2 teaspoons grated lemon rind

1 teaspoon vanilla essence

1½ cups red-skinned seedless grapes

1 cup Noble Riesling or other similar 'sticky'

Preheat the oven to 200°C.

Brush a 22cm loose-based cake pan with olive oil. Line the base and sides with baking paper and brush with olive oil again.

Sift the flour, salt and baking soda into a bowl.

Beat the butter, sugar and olive oil, until creamy. Beat in the eggs, lemon rind and vanilla.

Take 2 tablespoons of the flour mixture and dust over the grapes so they are lightly covered.

Fold the remainder of the flour into the butter mixture alternately with the Noble Riesling, mixing after each addition, until just smooth. Spoon the batter into the pan and sprinkle the grapes over the top.

Bake for about 45 minutes, until a skewer inserted in the centre comes out clean. Serve warm or at room temperature with whipped cream. **SERVES ABOUT 10.**

WINE MATCH

Definitely a Noble Riesling. Sweet, rich and weighty – the perfect accompaniment to this delicious cake.

Seafood Supreme

24 Kono Mussels in their shells

1 cup Sauvignon Blanc

8 sprigs fresh mixed herbs eg thyme, tarragon, fennel

300g groper (hapuku) or Regal Salmon Fillet

½ cup extra virgin olive oil

¼ cup Sauvignon Blanc vinegar

3 tablespoons grated root ginger

3 spring onions, slivered

Scrub the mussels and remove the beards. Place in a large saucepan with a ¼ cup each of wine and water. Cover and steam until the mussels are just opened. Stir once during cooking.

Combine the remaining wine and the herbs. Bring to the boil in a frying pan. Discard the bones and skin from the fish and cut the flesh in 24 pieces about the same size as the mussels. Place in the wine mixture and poach for a few minutes, until just cooked. Drain.

Remove the mussels from their shells leaving the shells joined at the base. Place the mussels and salmon in a bowl. Combine the oil, vinegar, ginger and spring onions and pour over the fish. Marinate in the refrigerator for at least 2 hours.

To serve, place a mussel and a piece of salmon in each mussel shell. Top with a little of the marinade, the ginger and spring onions. Serve in shallow bowls with crusty bread.
SERVES 4.

WINE MATCH

With Sauvignon Blanc used in the cooking of this dish, it would certainly be a good partner to enjoy alongside it. Off-dry Riesling would also work and even an off-dry style of Pinot Gris, which would also give a more textural match.

Verjuice

Verjuice adds excellent flavour to salad dressings and sauces in place of lemon juice or vinegar.

To make, choose 1kg of Sauvignon Blanc or Pinot Noir grapes that are just starting to colour. Remove the stalks and place the grapes in a food processor. Pulse until the grapes are coarsely crushed.

Place a double layer of muslin in a coarse strainer over a large bowl. Strain the crushed grapes through the muslin. This will take a couple of hours.

Discard the crushed grapes and strain the liquid through clean muslin twice to remove any sediment.

Place the liquid in a saucepan. Add 2 tablespoons of sugar and bring to the boil. Remove from the heat. If the liquid is still cloudy then you can add a lightly beaten egg white and stir it slowly until it is clearer. Strain again. Bring to the boil and either seal in small jars or pour into ice cube trays and freeze. **MAKES ABOUT 1 CUP.**

Summer evening,
Seymour Square,
Blenheim

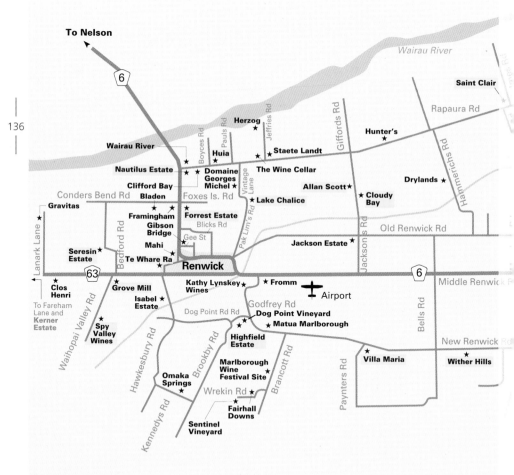

WINE
MARLBOROUGH
NEW ZEALAND

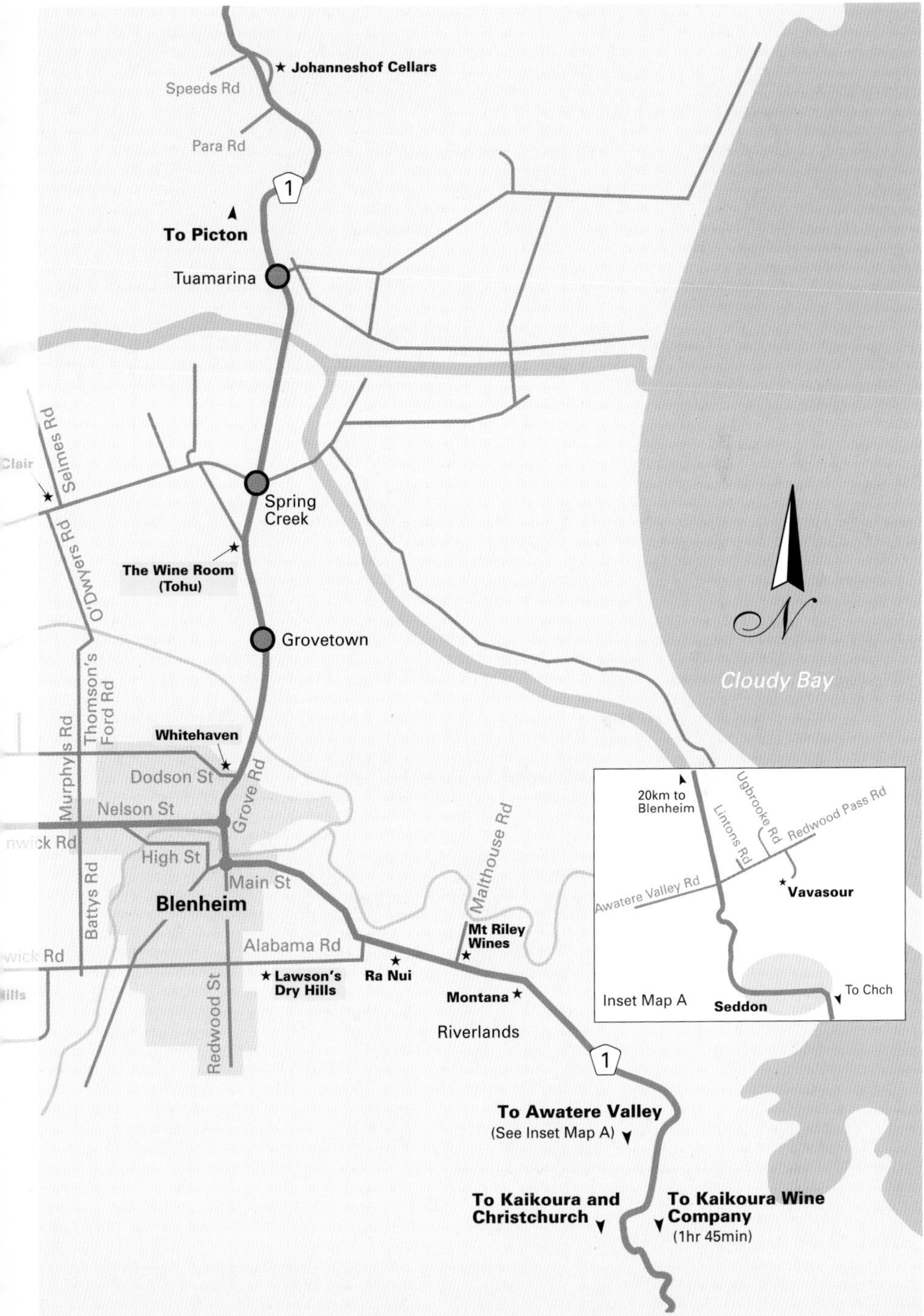

★ Johanneshof Cellars

Speeds Rd

Para Rd

1

To Picton

Tuamarina

Spring
Creek

★
The Wine Room
(Tohu)

Grovetown

Clair
★

Selmes Rd

O'Dwyers Rd

Thomson's
Ford Rd

Murphys Rd

Whitehaven
★
Dodson St
Nelson St

nwick Rd

Battys Rd

High St

Grove Rd

Main St
Blenheim

Alabama Rd

wick Rd

Redwood St

★ Lawson's
Dry Hills

Ra Nui
★

ills

Malthouse Rd

Mt Riley
Wines
★

Montana ★

Riverlands

1

Cloudy Bay

Inset Map A

20km to
Blenheim

Ugbrooke Rd

Lintons Rd

Redwood Pass Rd

Awatere Valley Rd

★
Vavasour

To Chch

Seddon

N

To Awatere Valley
(See Inset Map A) ▼

**To Kaikoura and
Christchurch** ▼

▼ **To Kaikoura Wine
Company**
(1hr 45min)

Allan Scott Family Winemakers
& Twelve Trees Restaurant
Jackson's Rd, RD3
Blenheim 7273
www.allanscott.com
03 572 9054

Astrolabe Wines
PO Box 1152, Blenheim 7240
www.astrolabewines.co.nz
03 577 6794

**Cloudy Bay Winery
& Cellar Door**
PO Box 376, Blenheim 7240
Jackson's Rd, Blenheim
www.cloudybay.co.nz
03 520 9147

Forrest Estate
19 Blicks Rd
Renwick 7204
www.forrestwines.co.nz
03 572 9084

Grove Mill Winery
PO Box 67, Renwick 7243
Cnr Waihopai Valley Rd &
State Highway 63
Renwick
www.grovemill.co.nz
03 572 8200

Highfield Estate
Brookby Rd, RD2
Renwick 7272
www.highfield.co.nz
03 572 9244

Huia Vineyards
PO Box 92, Renwick 7243
Boyces Rd, Renwick
www.huia.net.nz
03 572 8326

Lake Chalice
PO Box 66, Renwick 7243
93 Vintage Lane, Renwick
www.lakechalice.com
03 572 9327

Lawson's Dry Hills
PO Box 4020,
Redwoodtown 7201
238 Alabama Rd, Blenheim
www.lawsonsdryhills.co.nz
03 578 7674

Nautilus Estate
PO Box 107, Renwick 7243
12 Rapaura Rd, Renwick
www.nautilusestate.com
03 572 6008

No 1 Family Estate
169 Rapaura Rd
Rapaura, Blenheim 7273
www.no1familyestate.co.nz
03 572 9876

Seresin Estate
PO Box 859, Blenheim 7240
85 Bedford Rd, Renwick
www.seresin.co.nz
03 572 9408

Saint Clair Family Estate
PO Box 970, Blenheim 7240
Saint Clair Café & Cellar Door
13 Selmes Rd, Rapaura, Blenheim
www.saintclair.co.nz
03 570 5280

Spy Valley
37 Lake Timara Rd, RD 6
Blenheim 7276
www.spyvalley.co.nz
03 572 9840

Te Whare Ra
PO Box 70, Renwick 7243
56 Anglesea St, Renwick
www.tewharera.co.nz
03 572 8581

Tohu Wines
PO Box 1028, Blenheim 7240
The Wine Room, State Highway 1
Grovetown, Blenheim
www.tohu.co.nz
03 520 9320

Villa Maria Estate
PO Box 848, Blenheim 7240
Cnr Paynters & New Renwick Rds
Fairhall, Blenheim
www.villamaria.co.nz
03 520 8470

Whitehaven Wine Company
39 Pauls Rd, RD3, Rapaura, 7273
Whitehaven Cellar Door &
Conservatory Restaurant
1 Dodson St, Blenheim
www.whitehaven.co.nz
03 577 6634

Wither Hills
211 New Renwick Rd, RD2
Blenheim 7272
www.witherhills.co.nz
03 520 8270

Cheese
Sherrington Grange Ltd
Mahu Sound, RD2
Picton 7282
www.sherringtongrange.co.nz
03 574 2655

Cherries
Sujon Berryfruits Ltd
17 Bullen St, Tahunanui
Nelson 7001
www.sujon.co.nz
03 546 4306

Farmed Venison
Silver Fern Venison
PO Box 941, Dunedin 9054
www.silverfernfarms.co.nz
03 477 3980

Flaky Sea Salt
Pacific Salt Marlborough Flaky Sea Salt
Cerebos Greggs Ltd
PO Box 58095
Greenmount, Manukau 2141
www.dominionsalt.co.nz
09 274 2777

Garlic & Shallots
NZ Garlic & NZ Shallots
Phoenix Garlic Company Ltd
PO Box 5146, Blenheim 7241
377 Vickerman St, Grovetown
www.nzgarlic.co.nz
03 577 8547

Gourmet Vinegars & Flavours & Infused Rice-bran Oils
Prenzel Distilling Co Ltd
PO Box 246, Blenheim 7240
Sheffield St,
Riverlands Estate &
193 Rapaura Rd, Blenheim
www.prenzel.com
03 520 8215

Herbs & Salad Greens
Thymebank (2005) Ltd
31 Hammerichs Rd
Blenheim 7272
03 577 9499

Mussels
Kono New Zealand
Aotearoa Seafoods Ltd
PO Box 762, Blenheim 7240
16 Bristol Street, Blenheim
www.kono.co.nz
03 520 9212

Olive Oil
Blumenfeld Olive Oil Ltd
PO Box 876, Blenheim 7240
20 Bomford St, Blenheim
www.blumenfeld.co.nz
03 577 9834

Oysters
Talleys Group Ltd
PO Box 5
Motueka, Nelson 7143
www.talleys.co.nz
03 528 2869

Saffron
Gourmet Gold Ltd
21 Lakings Rd, Blenheim 7201
www.gopurmetgoldsaffron.co.nz
03 578 3793

Salmon
Regal Salmon
NZ King Salmon Ltd
PO Box 12957
Penrose, Auckland 1642
www.regalsalmon.co.nz
09 526 7642

Walnuts & Hazelnuts
Uncle Joe's Walnuts
39 Rowley Cres,
Grovetown 7202
www.unclejoes.co.nz
03 577 9884

Wild Game
Premium Game Ltd
PO Box 1059, Blenheim 7240
49 Bristol Street, Blenheim
www.game-meats.co.nz
03 577 8200

HINTS

Weights & Measures
Recipes in this book use standard, level, metric measurements.

In New Zealand, England and the USA 1 tablespoon equals 15ml. In Australia, 1 tablespoon equals 20ml. The variation will not normally greatly affect the result of a recipe apart from some bakes and cakes.

If preferred, use 3 teaspoons rather than 1 Australian tablespoon for measures of raising agents and spices.

Grams to Ounces
These are converted to the nearest measurable number.

grams		ounces	grams		ounces
25	=	1	275	=	10
50	=	2	300	=	10.5
75	=	3	325	=	11
100	=	3.5	350	=	12
125	=	4	375	=	13
150	=	5	400	=	14
175	=	6	425	=	15
200	=	7	450	=	16
225	=	8	1kg = 1000g = 2lb 4oz		
250	=	9			

Abbreviations
Metric

g	grams
kg	kilograms
mm	millimetre
cm	centimetre
ml	millilitre
°C	degree Celsius

Oven Setting Equivalents (To Nearest 10°C)

	Fahrenheit	Celsius	Gas regulo No
Very cool	225-275	110-140	1/4-1
Cool	300-325	150-160	2-3
Moderate	350-375	180-190	4-5
Hot	400-450	200-230	6-8
Very hot	475-500	250-260	9-10

Cup & Spoon Measures
(to nearest round number)

	Metric
¼ cup	60ml
½ cup	125ml
1 cup	250ml
2 cups	500ml
4 cups	1000ml or 1 litre
1 teaspoon	5ml
1 dessertspoon	10ml
1 tablespoon	15ml
2 teaspoons	1 dessertspoon
3 teaspoons	1 tablespoon
16 tablespoons	1 cup

Measures of Length

cm		approx. inches	cm		approx. inches
0.5	=	¼	18	=	7
1	=	½	20	=	8
2.5	=	1	23	=	9
5	=	2	25	=	10
15	=	6	30	=	12

Alternative Names
In the English-speaking world, many culinary terms and names of foods cross national borders without creating confusion. However, some may need explanation.

cake pan	cake tin/baking pan
caster sugar	castor sugar/ fine granulated sugar/superfine sugar
coriander	cilantro/Chinese parsley
cornflour	cornstarch
crayfish	rock lobster
eggplant	aubergine
essence	extract
flour	plain flour/all-purpose flour
frying pan	skillet
grill	broil
groper	hapuku
icing sugar	confectioners'/powdered sugar
minced meat	ground meat
peppers	capsicums/sweet peppers
poussin	spatchcock
rocket	arugula/roquette
rockmelon	cantaloupe
sieve	strain
spring onions	scallions/green onions
to stone	pit
tomato paste	concentrated tomato paste
tomato purée	tomato sauce (USA)

The magical Marlborough Sounds

INDEX